Picture acknowledgements:
All-Sport; Associated Press; Barnabys Picture Library;
BBC Hulton Picture Library; Central Press; Colorsport;
Gerry Cranham; Patrick Eagar; Fox Photos; Ray Green;
Keystone Press Agency; Ed Lacey; Neil Leifer/Sports
Illustrated (Time Life); the Mansell Collection;
Leo Mason; the National Motor Museum; Popperfoto;
the Press Association; Peter Robinson/Mick Alexander;
Sporting Pictures (UK); Syndication International;
Visnews; Yorkshire Post

GREAT MOMENTS IN SPORT

Norman Barrett

Editor   Deborah Brammer
Designer   Ruth Hall

ISBN 0 361 05307 X

Copyright © 1982 Purnell Publishers Limited
Published 1982 by Purnell Books,
Paulton, Bristol, BS18 5LQ
Made and printed in Great Britain by
Purnell and Sons (Book Production) Limited,
Paulton, Bristol

Purnell

Contents

Introduction

Sport provides us with some of the most stirring moments of our lives, whether we are participating ourselves or thrilling to the deeds of others. In a world where 'No news is good news', the sports news provides us with an escape. We can enjoy the exploits of finely trained athletes as they strive to come out on top or to push back the barriers of achievement a little further. We can sit back in our armchairs while the excitement of a World Cup or an Olympic Games is beamed to us live by satellite, or we can go out and shout from the terraces for our local team. Great sporting moments come in all shapes and sizes. They are provided by winners and losers, artists and heroes, favourites and underdogs.

At the top level, however, sport has become too important, the need to win — by whatever means — too much a doctrine. We cannot return to the days of the 'gentleman amateur'; we would not want to. But modern sport, sadly, suffers from many ailments, from chauvinism to drug abuse, from greed to violence both on and off the field. In many sports, sponsorship and the needs of television have taken over. Sport is in danger of losing its identity. The days of *Rollerball* and *Death Race 2000* are not far off.

All these trends must be reversed. Nationalism in sport must not be allowed to destroy goodwill. The individual athlete must strike a balance between winning and sportsmanship. The truly great sportsman is the one who wins in style, not the one who wins at all costs. Here's to the Pelés and Comptons, the Zatopeks and Barry Johns, the Mary Peters and Evonne Goolagongs. This book is dedicated to them.

Norman Barrett

Billy Meredith

W. G. Grace

Baron Coubertin

Jim Thorpe

Jack Johnson

Lottie Dod

Fred Archer

C. W. Alcock

THE EARLY DAYS

The Ancient Greeks were the first to establish the great sporting spectacle, with their Olympics and other sporting celebrations some 3,000 years ago. There was very little sport in the Middle Ages, although combat sports such as wrestling and the martial arts were to be found in most societies. But it was not until the 1800s that organized sport as we know it today first took hold — in the English universities.

In the 20th century, competitive sport began to flourish, thanks to the vision and industry of such men as Baron Coubertin, 'father' of the modern Olympics, and Charles Alcock, who not only founded the FA Cup, but captained the first winners. Alcock also set up the first soccer international (only injury prevented his taking part as England's captain) and the first cricket Test to be played in England.

Great personalities emerged in many sports — the heroes and the villains. They included W. G. Grace, who dominated the cricketing scene with his personality as well as his unmatched all-round ability; the immensely popular and tragic jockey Fred Archer; Captain Matthew Webb, the first man to swim the Channel; Jim Thorpe, arguably the outstanding all-round sportsman of all time; the first great woman all-rounder, Lottie Dod, youngest ever Wimbledon champion and golf and hockey international; cricketer, footballer, and athlete C. B. Fry; Welsh wing wizard Billy Meredith, whose footballing career spanned four decades; and one of the finest — and most hated — of heavyweight champions, Jack Johnson.

WORLD EVENTS IN THE EARLY DAYS ...Greek and Roman civilizations...birth of Christ

...Renaissance...works of Shakespeare... man's first flight...World War I...........

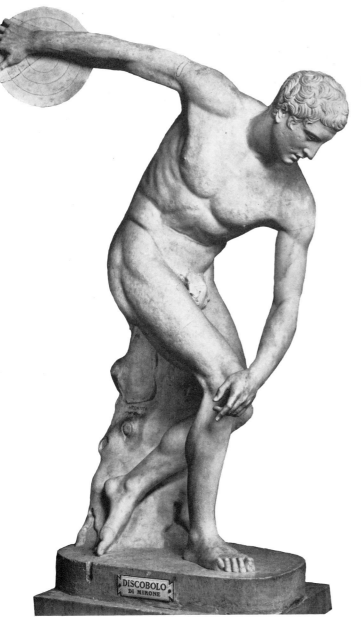

'Local boy' wins first Olympics

The first 'great moments in sport' took place in Ancient Greece, where there were many celebrations and festivals in which athletics contests featured. The most famous of these ritual 'games' was that held at the temple of Zeus in Olympia. The year 776 BC marks the start of the Ancient Olympics. They were held every four years, and lasted for over a thousand years.

The Ancient Games grew from a single event, the 'stade' race (the length of the stadium — nearly 200 metres), to a five-day festival that included boxing, chariot racing, races in armour, a long-distance race, and a no-holds-barred combat event called the 'pankration', in which contestants were often seriously injured or even killed. There was also the five-event pentathlon — long jump, javelin, discus, sprint, and wrestling.

Olympic victors were fêted as great heroes, earning undying fame in their native lands and 'immortality' after death. The first recorded triumph — perhaps the first great moment in sport — was that of Coroebus of Elis, the 'local boy' who won the stade race in 776 BC.

Left: Discobolus, a sculpture that shows all the grace and beauty of the Ancient Greek discus thrower.

Below: Crowds brave the rain to watch the great running match in 1852, held over 10 miles.

'Great running match'

Footracing became popular in England as long ago as the 1660s. The professionals, who became known as 'pedestrians', attracted huge crowds as well as a great deal of betting. Most of the early contests were between footmen, who were employed to carry messages over the poor roads of the 1700s. Pedestrians continued to flourish well into the late 1800s, and there were some memorable races.

One such event took place in January 1852, when 'nearly all the pedestrians of celebrity were brought together' in London's Copenhagen Fields. Some 5,000 gathered to witness the 'great running match', in which the winner, Frost, recorded a creditable 54 minutes 21 seconds for 10 miles over wet ground.

The First Grand National

A ducking for Captain Becher earns him immortality

The first Grand National, and Captain Becher (bottom left, in yellow) takes refuge in the brook that took his name. The winner, seen in the centre taking the obstacle confidently, was called Lottery.

The first Grand National took place in and around the little Lancashire village of Aintree on February 26, 1839. The race was organized by a syndicate of local men, notably the Liverpool publican William Lynn. The race was held on ploughed land with 29 'fences', natural boundaries between fields which could be jumped wherever the rider chose.

More than one of these barriers was a brook, and at the first brook a rider fell off his horse, Conrad, and took shelter by diving into the brook to evade the hooves of following horses. The name of the rider was Captain Becher, and he gave his name to the obstacle. Over the years 'Becher's Brook' has been the downfall of countless National hopefuls.

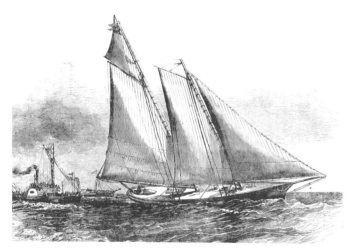

'There is no second'

Above left: The Yacht *America* in the historic race at Cowes in 1851.

Dead Heat

In 1851, the New York Yacht Club sent the 170-ton schooner *America* to challenge Britain's best for a 100-guinea silver cup presented by the Royal Yacht Squadron. On August 22, seven schooners and eight cutters set out from Cowes to uphold the honour of British yachting in the race round the Isle of Wight. *America* crossed the finishing line 18 minutes ahead of her closest rival. When Queen Victoria, aboard the royal yacht, asked who won, the reply was: '*America* first, Your Majesty; there is no second.'

Above right: An artist's impression of the finish of the 1877 University Boat Race, when there occurred the only dead heat in the history of the event.

This historic race turned out to be the forerunner of the America's Cup, when the trophy was later put up for challenge. Some 130 years later and after more than 25 challenges (latterly from other countries as well as Britain), none has been able to relieve the New York Yacht Club of the problem of cleaning the Cup.

The University Boat Race is a great national tradition in England. A contest between eights of Cambridge and Oxford, it first took place in 1829, and has been held annually since 1856, with the exception of the war years.

In some years, the race is a 'procession' over the sinewy 4¼ miles of the Thames from Putney to Mortlake. But there have been some classic contests, and perhaps the greatest of these was the one that took place in 1877, when the crews could not be separated at the finish.

The First Channel Swim

Webb helped ashore at Calais.

Swim the English Channel? They said it couldn't be done. But, as with all feats deemed by the 'experts' to be impossible, there is always a man or woman of great courage and determination ready to accept the ultimate challenge. Such a man was Matthew Webb, a captain in the Merchant Navy.

On August 24, 1875, Captain Webb set out from Admiralty Pier, Dover, on his historic swim. He had made an unsuccessful attempt 12 days earlier, when rough seas had forced him to give up half-way across. This time, however, the water was calmer. But he had the tides and currents to contend with, and his zigzag route eventually took him an estimated 63km, some 30km more than

the shortest distance across the Channel. Breast-stroking his way through the water, with the occasional rest on his back, Webb was sustained with coffee, brandy, and beef tea. He arrived at Calais on August 25, after 21 hours and 45 minutes in the water, to a tremendous reception, and he became a national hero. It was another 36 years before man conquered the Channel again.

Fred Archer–the Backers' Best Friend

The finest and most popular jockey of the 19th century, Fred Archer was only 29 when he died in 1886. He had been champion jockey for 13 consecutive seasons and won 2,748 of his 8,084 races — a remarkable record. He won 21 Classics, including five Derbies.

Perhaps his most memorable race was on Bend Or in the 1880 Derby. Riding virtually one-handed — his other arm had been savaged by a loose horse some weeks earlier — he got his mount up to win at the post in a typically courageous finish. No wonder they called him 'the backers' best friend'.

Archer drives Bend Or to the line.

First International

The first official soccer match between two countries took place in Glasgow on November 30, 1872, between Scotland and England. This was an auspicious occasion, for it set the tradition not only of the England–Scotland fixture but of worldwide international football. An estimated 3,000 to 4,000 spectators paid £109 to see the goalless draw.

Twins fight out first five-set final

Willie and Ernie Renshaw were twin brothers, born in 1861. They dominated lawn tennis in the 1880s and are regarded as creators of the modern game. The 'Renshaw smash' was spoken of in awe and their volleying was equally famous. Their skill and personality turned the game into a spectator sport.

The first Wimbledon championship was held in 1877, and in the early days the holder of the title was challenged by the winner of all the other entrants. Willie Renshaw won his first title in 1881, beating the holder the Rev. J. T. Hartley 6-0, 6-2, 6-1 in 37 minutes, still the fastest men's singles final. In 1882 he beat his brother Ernie in the first five-set final, 6-1, 2-6, 4-6, 6-2, 6-2.

Above: **An artist who did not appreciate the need for players to keep their eyes on the ball depicts the 1882 Wimbledon final.**
Left: **A contemporary artist's impression of the first international, played at the West of Scotland Cricket Ground, Partick. The match was described as 'A splendid display of football'.**

Out of the ashes . . .

The first England–Australia cricket match took place in Melbourne in 1877, and before long the series of 'Test' matches between the two countries assumed an importance it has never lost. When Australia won the only match in England in 1882, it was regarded in the home country as a national disaster, and a mock obituary notice appeared the next day in the *Sporting Times*:

> In affectionate remembrance
> of
> English Cricket
> which died at the Oval on
> 29th August, 1882,
> deeply lamented by a large circle of
> sorrowing friends and acquaintances
> R.I.P.
> N.B. The body will be cremated and
> the Ashes taken to Australia

In a low-scoring match, one of the most exciting ever played, England had been set 85 runs to win in the last innings. Thanks to a superb spell of bowling by F. R. Spofforth, 'the demon bowler', they failed by eight runs. Spofforth, who three years earlier at Melbourne had taken 13 England wickets for 110, including the first ever Test hat-trick, produced another devastating performance with seven wickets in each innings for a total of 90 runs.

The following winter England won the Test series in Australia. After the deciding match, some ladies burnt a stump, sealed its ashes in an urn, and presented it to the English captain, the Hon. Ivo Bligh. Thus began the great tradition of 'the Ashes'.

The urn that holds the legendary Ashes stands permanently in the Memorial Gallery at Lord's, even when Australia 'holds' them.

End of an era

Bare-knuckle fighting developed as an art in England, and was immensely popular in the 1700s and 1800s. Wealthy aristocrats sponsored the best of the 'pugilists' and wagered huge sums on the outcome of a fight. Gloves were introduced in the mid-1800s, but bare-knuckle bouts continued to draw the crowds for several years.

An American, John L. Sullivan, beat all and sundry, and earned himself the title of heavyweight champion of the world. His finest performance was against challenger Jake Kilrain at Richburg, Mississippi, in 1889. He emerged the victor after an epic contest that lasted 75 rounds and 2¾ hours. This fight also marked the end of an era, for it was the last heavyweight battle under prize-ring rules. Three years later, an out-of-condition Sullivan put on gloves and lost his title to 'Gentleman Jim' Corbett.

Sullivan (right) v Kilrain, with Mississippi Rangers to keep the peace. Kilrain's corner threw in the sponge after 75 rounds.

Preston achieve 'double' undefeated

The 'double' is a term in English football that really stirs the emotions. It refers to the winning of both League and Cup in the same season. It has been such a rare feat that at one time it was thought impossible in modern football in England, where the competition is so keen and the season so strenuous. Yet it was accomplished in the very first season of the Football League.

The team that achieved this pinnacle of performance was Preston North End, the first of the great professional sides. They did it in style, winning the Championship without losing a game (won 18, drew 4) and the Cup without conceding a goal.

This achievement in the early days of organized football might be belittled by those accustomed to the intensity of modern competition. But the deeds of 'Proud Preston' are not easily brushed aside. More than 40 years after that historic 1888–89 season, they were still spoken of in awe and regarded by many experts as the greatest side of all time.

Preston conceded only 15 goals in their 22 League games, but it was their goalscoring power that marked them as the great side they undoubtedly were. Led by the legendary John Goodall (21 goals), the acknowledged pioneer of scientific soccer in England, they scored 74. They finished 11 points clear of Aston Villa in the League, and beat Wolves 3–0 in the Cup final. Preston's double has since been emulated in much more difficult circumstances, but no team has ever gone through an English season undefeated. No wonder they called them 'the Invincibles'.

Greek wins first marathon

The hero of the first modern Olympic Games, staged in Athens, was a Greek, Spiridon Louis. The marathon was a long-distance endurance test to commemorate the famous feat in 490 BC of the Greek soldier Pheidippides. He is said to have carried news of a famous victory 25 miles from Marathon to Athens before dying from exhaustion. In 1896, the marathon was the last of the athletics events, and as none of the previous events had been won by the host country, all hopes were pinned on this race.

Local 'sponsors' promised the winner, if Greek, a variety of rewards, ranging from jewellery to free haircuts for life. Louis did not disappoint them. He outlasted the 16 other runners to win by 7min 13sec (still a record winning margin). The race not only climaxed a highly successful first modern Olympics, but set a pattern for the many dramatic marathons to come.

An artist's impression of the finish of the first Olympic marathon, at Athens in 1896.

The first great miler

Walter George (caricatured above) dominated middle- and long-distance running in the 1880s. The champion of champions, he set world records at 1 to 10 miles and for the hour run. He broke a dozen world records as an amateur, before turning professional in 1884.

George had brought the world mile record down to 4min 18.4sec, some 6 seconds better than the old record. But William Cummings, a Scottish professional, had a best time of 4min 16.2 sec. The AAA refused George permission to race Cummings, so he turned professional. Their first clash, in August 1885, drew a 30,000 crowd, and George won easing up in 4min 20.2sec. A year later, on August 23, came the race for which George is best remembered. He again eclipsed the Scot, and broke the tape in 4min 12¾sec, a time unsurpassed for 29 years and one of the most outstanding sporting feats of the 19th century.

Against All Odds

From wheelchair to Olympic immortality

The outstanding performer of the 1900 Olympic Games was Ray Ewry, an American who won three gold medals. Three Olympic titles is a fine achievement by any standards, but to appreciate the magnitude of his feat you have to go back to his childhood. For as a boy, Ewry was paralysed, and confined to a wheelchair. The doctors said he would never walk again. He refused to accept this, however, and devised exercises that eventually developed exceptionally powerful legs. He won the three standing jumps (high, long, and triple), performed from a stationary position. In later Olympics, this remarkable athlete went on to amass eight individual gold medals, still a record in any sport.

Former cripple Ray Ewry winning the standing high jump at the 1900 Olympics in Paris.

14

The Great Marathon Hoax

The first Olympics to be held outside Europe were staged in St Louis in 1904. They were dominated by American competitors, partly because few European nations could afford to send full-strength teams across the Atlantic. The star of the Games was American sprinter Archie Hahn, who won the 60m, 100m, and 200m gold medals. But the man who made the most impact was marathon runner Fred Lorz.

The marathon field consisted mainly of Americans and Greeks. They had to contend with a hilly 40km course, a temperature in the nineties, and choking clouds of thick dust and exhaust fumes thrown up by the accompanying vehicles. Lorz retired with cramp during the race and accepted a lift. But the car broke down. Feeling fitter now, he decided to run the last few kilometres back to the stadium to collect his clothes.

When he arrived, he was hailed as the winner, and stepped up to receive his victor's wreath before he was denounced as a fraud.

Meanwhile, another American, British-born Thomas Hicks, was staggering over the last few kilometres, sustained by eggs, brandy, and doses of strychnine administered by his four attendants. He nearly collapsed when the refreshed Lorz passed him full of running! But he revived when persuaded that Lorz was no longer in the race, and went on to win by six minutes.

Lorz's impromptu 'hoax' landed him a life suspension, but he was reinstated after a year. Hicks survived an objection to his on-course assistance. And another runner almost died from inhaling so much abrasive dust. The Olympic marathon was fast earning a reputation for sensation.

The winner of the 1904 marathon, Thomas Hicks, is pictured receiving attention from two of his attendants three kilometres from the finish. He nearly collapsed when 'hiker' Lorz passed him full of running, and had to be persuaded to continue. Hicks survived an objection to his on-course attention, but in view of what was to happen in 1908, he was lucky.

The all-conquering All Blacks

The first New Zealand rugby side to tour Britain arrived in 1905 an unknown quantity — so much so that when they thrashed English County Champions Devon 55–4 in their first match, few people believed the result. Some newspapers questioned the score when it was flashed through and reversed the figures!

There was no mistake, however, and the all-conquering All Blacks proceeded to sweep all opposition aside. Forty-point victories were commonplace. They won 32 of their 33 matches, with a points aggregate of 868 against 47.

Their only loss was 3–0 to Wales. In the dying minutes, All Black centre Bob Deans had a try disallowed for falling short of the line — New Zealanders say he was dragged back. The controversy lingers to this day.

Gordon Bennett!

The 1903 race for the Gordon Bennett Cup was the first motor race held in Great Britain. An American newspaper tycoon, Bennett had donated a trophy to promote international racing in 1900, the event to be held in the country of the club winning the previous year's race.

As the 1902 event was won by a British car, the authorities had a problem. Racing was prohibited on the roads of England, Scotland, and Wales. The Irish authorities gave their consent, however, and the race took place on a triangular section of closed roads at Athy, in County Kildare. It was won by a Belgian in a German car, a Mercedes.

Belgian driver Camille Jenatzy is hailed as victor of the 1903 Gordon Bennett race, the first motor race held in Great Britain.

The Dorando Marathon

Gallant Italian disqualified — but who remembers the winner?

The 1908 Olympics were held in London, and the marathon began at Windsor Castle and finished with three-fifths of a lap at the White City Stadium. Italian sweet-maker Dorando Pietri (known as Dorando because that was how his name appeared on the programme) became the hero of the Games even though he failed to win a medal. Of all the dramatic marathons before and since 1908, the 'Dorando marathon' stands out. The British public always loves an underdog, and there was more than a touch of Charlie Chaplin about the Italian.

He came to the Games with a high reputation as a distance runner, but he also had a history of bad luck and was prone to confusion. It was said that his running career began by accident, when as a 17-year-old he ran an errand, delivering a letter in person instead of posting it, and covering nearly 50km in about four hours in the process!

A diminutive, bandy-legged figure, moustachioed and wearing long, bright red shorts, he was prominent throughout the race. He reached the stadium first, but was almost unconscious as he stumbled onto the track. True to form, he began to go the wrong way (the normal direction had been reversed). He collapsed on the track, and doctors and attendants rushed to his assistance. Partially revived, he began to lurch towards the tape, a pathetic figure now, falling down every few steps but each time picking himself up with tremendous courage and determination. The crowd were willing him on, but he had to be helped up several times, and staggered across the line aided by officials. The assistance he received automatically disqualified him.

Half a minute later, a 19-year-old American, John Hayes, finished and was awarded the race. Dorando received a special gold cup from Queen Alexandra. He also won the hearts of the public and earned sporting immortality. After all, who remembers the name of the winner?

Right: **Italian marathon runner Dorando Pietri staggers towards the finishing line with anxious officials lending a hand.**

Birth of a New Sport

Brooklands — the first motor race meeting

On July 6, 1907, a new sport was born. The Brooklands racetrack, at Weybridge, Surrey, was the first circuit anywhere in the world to be specifically built for motor racing. Thus motor sport was taken off the roads onto the track. The 4.4km raceway was constructed of concrete, with turns banked higher than a house. Brooklands aroused great public enthusiasm from the start. For that first meeting, there were six events offering a total of £5,000 prize money — a huge sum in those days. And to cap it all, one of the races finished in a dead heat.

Two cars scream round the last turn to dead-heat at the finish.

The Fight of the Century

Jack Johnson thrashes 'great white hope'

Jack Johnson and James J. Jeffries would both feature high on anyone's list of the world's all-time great heavyweights. So when they met on July 4, 1910, in Reno, it was one of the most eagerly awaited bouts in the history of boxing.

Jack Johnson was a highly controversial character, the 'Muhammad Ali' of his time. In those days, Negro fighters were tolerated only when they were beaten. For over ten years Johnson had defeated most of the contenders, but with little chance of a crack at the title. But he followed champion Tommy Burns on a world tour, caught up with him in 1908 in Australia, and battered him to defeat in 14 rounds.

As the first black heavyweight champion, he became the most hated man in the United States, although much of this was due to his arrogance. The search began for a 'great white hope' to win back the heavyweight crown. Finally, the great champion Jim Jeffries, who had twice accounted for both Bob Fitzsimmons and Jim Corbett in an undefeated career, was persuaded to come out of retirement.

Jeffries was now 35, six years out of the ring and 45kg overweight. But he put up a determined show against all the odds before finally succumbing in the 15th round.

Left: Scenes from the fight.
Below: The end for Jeffries.

A Record Break

Billiards champion Tom Reece from Oldham compiled an unfinished break of 499,135 in 1907. Having manoeuvred the two object balls into the jaws of a corner pocket, he proceeded to play his 'anchor cannon' for five weeks, a total of 86 hours at the table, while his helpless opponent looked on.

The Colossus of Cricket

William Gilbert Grace bestrode the world of cricket like a colossus for nearly 40 years from the late 1860s. A large man and heavily bearded from an early age, he dominated the game with his personality, formidable appearance, and all-round cricketing skills. He was a truly national figure.

'W.G.' made his first-class debut in 1865 at 17, for the Gentlemen, and was still representing them 40 years later. He qualified as a doctor at 31, and rarely

Great Moments in W.G.'s career

1871 2,739 runs in season (all strokes run out)
First-class average 78.25 (next man averaged 34)
1873 10–92 in innings for MCC
1876 344 for MCC, 177 and 318 not out for Glos., all in eight days
1877 17–89 in match for Glos.
1880 152 v Australia on Test debut (first English hundred in Tests)
1886 10–49 in innings for MCC
1895 1,000 runs in May (first man to accomplish feat, and this at nearly 47!)

made overseas tours with England. He made his Test debut in 1880, at 32, scoring a hundred against Australia at the Oval. Two of his brothers — F.M. and G.F. — also played in this match. W.G. captained England for the first time in 1888, at 40, and led them in his last Test match in 1899, when he was over 50.

As an all-rounder, his career record is matchless. In first-class cricket, he scored 54,896 runs (5th best of all time), took 2,876 wickets (6th) and 877 catches (2nd), and made 126 hundreds (8th). He was still playing good club cricket at 66, a year before he died.

The Greatest

. . . but they took away his medals

The spectators at the 1912 Olympic Games in Stockholm were treated to one of the most extraordinary all-round performances in the history of sport. Jim Thorpe — part American Indian, part French and Irish — won both the decathlon and the pentathlon. He was head and shoulders above the other competitors, winning the 10-event decathlon by a huge points margin, and in the pentathlon taking first place in four of the five events. King Gustav of Sweden handed him his gold medals with the words: 'Sir, you are the greatest athlete in the world.'

He was the superman of sport, his exploits the stuff of schoolboy fiction. Soon after the Games he beat the Olympic high hurdles champion and equalled the world record. Yet the following year he had his medals taken away and his name expunged from the record books. He had apparently once received a few dollars for playing baseball during a college vacation, and the US Amateur Athletic Union ruled that this had infringed his amateur status.

Thorpe later earned further fame as a baseball star and then as a professional footballer — one of the 'all-time greats'. Sadly, he died in poverty in 1953, but not before he had been honoured in a Press poll as the greatest sportsman of the first half of the century. He was later immortalized on the screen as *Man of Bronze*, with Burt Lancaster playing the leading role.

Thorpe high-jumping at Stockholm.

First of the 'Flying Finns'

The 1912 Olympics marked the emergence of little Finland as a power in world athletics. And the man who made the rest of the world sit up with his performances in the long-distance events was Hannes Kolehmainen.

'Hannes the Mighty', as he became known, won three gold medals — in the 5,000m, 10,000m, and 8,000m cross-country. He won the 10,000m by over three-quarters of a minute, but the 5,000m was a tremendous race. Kolehmainen and Frenchman Jean Bouin dropped the rest of the field and fought out an epic duel before the Finn edged in front on the line. They both beat the previous world record by 25 seconds.

Finns won three field events, and Kolehmainen's elder brother Tatu came third in the marathon. In the next Olympics, in 1920, Hannes, at 31, won the marathon. He was the first of a remarkable band of Finnish athletes who became known as the 'Flying Finns' for their exploits on the tracks of the world.

Hannes Kolehmainen breasts the tape a stride ahead of Bouin to win the 1912 Olympic 5,000m.

Against All Odds

The 'Rorke's Drift' Test

Any student of British Colonial history — or anyone who has seen the film *Zulu* — will know that Rorke's Drift was a heroic battle in the Zulu War, when a handful of British soldiers repulsed thousands of Zulu warriors. A rugby league test match played in Sydney in 1914, when the Great Britain side courageously overcame overwhelming odds to beat Australia, has gone down in sporting history as the 'Rorke's Drift' test.

The British party arrived to tour Australia on the eve of World War I. When the third and final test was due, with the rubber 1–1, they were so beset with injuries that full-back Alf Wood had to play with a broken nose. Despite this and other knocks, Britain led 9–3 at half-time. Then, early in the second half, they lost three players in quick succession. But the ten men left proceeded to run the 13 Australians off their feet. Inspired by skipper Harold Wagstaff, they scored a try and ran out winners 14–6.

The Suffragette Derby

Woman killed throwing herself in front of King's horse

The most dramatic Derby of them all. Suffragette Emily Davison throws herself in front of the King's horse at Epsom in 1913. She died from her injuries. The race itself was one of the roughest, and one horse was disqualified. Women did not win the vote in Britain until 1918, and it was another ten years before they earned 'universal suffrage' (the vote at 21).

Barnes' Finest Hour

Medium-fast bowler Sydney Francis Barnes had a chequered career, playing mostly in the minor leagues. Yet he was regarded by some as the finest bowler of all time.

In the 1913–14 tour of South Africa, he took 49 wickets in only four Tests, still a record for a series. This included 17–159 in the second Test, a record that stood for over 40 years. He took five wickets in a Test innings a record 24 times.

His finest hour came in Australia, on December 30, 1911. In five overs before lunch at Melbourne in the second Test, he dismissed the cream of Australian batting — Bardsley, Kelleway, Hill, and Armstrong — for just cne run. He chalked up another scalp after lunch, and his bowling figures read: 11 overs, 7 maidens, 6 runs, 5 wickets. It was the turning-point of the series. Australia had won the first Test, but England went on to win the remaining four, Barnes contributing 34 wickets.

Suzanne Takes Wimbledon by Storm

. . . but she needs a fluke to dethrone champion

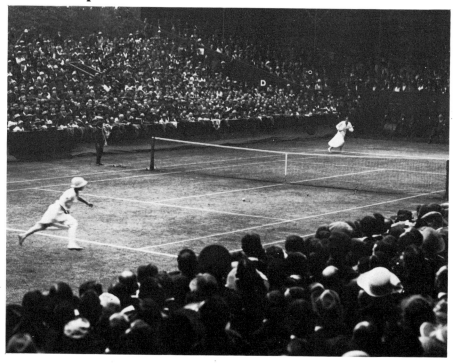

Of all the marvellous duels on Wimbledon's Centre Court over the years, the ladies' singles final of 1919 still ranks as one of the most exciting and dramatic. It was a classic confrontation between the old champion and the young challenger. Dorothea Lambert Chambers, now 40, had first won the title in 1903 as Miss Douglass and had won seven championships by the time World War I broke out. Suzanne Lenglen, half the champion's age, was on the threshold of her incomparable career, coming over from France with a fine reputation which she enhanced with the ease and fluency of her victories on the way to the challenge final, even though she had never played on grass before.

On the day of the encounter, Wimbledon was alive with anticipation. The public interest was so high that a record crowd crammed into the Centre Court. They were not disappointed. If appearances were anything to go by, the champion would not have had much hope. It looked like a carthorse–thoroughbred confrontation. And when the young, balletic Frenchwoman took the first set 10–8, there were few who gave the older woman a chance, and even fewer when she went 4–1 down in the second. Somehow, though, she kept

herself going, and it was Miss Lenglen who began to wilt, losing the next five games and the set.

Yet in the final set, she again swept into a 4–1 lead. And again the champion levelled at 4–4, and seemed to have it won at 6–5 and 40–15 — two match points. Then came a point that has gone down in tennis folklore, a fluke that was to determine the result of this dramatic see-saw match. Suzanne recklessly attacked the net on a short ball. Mrs

Lenglen (left) and Chambers in their 1919 Centre Court classic.

Chambers lobbed. The French girl flung up her racket in desperation, catching the ball on the top of the frame, and it fell onto the top of the net and dropped over. She went on to win the set 9–7. The champion was dethroned. Suzanne was the new queen of Wimbledon. It was to be a long and dazzling reign.

Other great moments and exploits of the early days

Lottie Dod won the ladies' singles at Wimbledon in 1887 — at 15 years 10 months the youngest ever to do so. She won the title five times in all, and played golf and hockey for England.

Gilbert Jessop hit a hundred in 75 minutes, the fastest Test century for England. Coming in when England were 48–5 against the Australians at the Oval in 1902, and needing another 215 to win, he hit 104 out of 139 in 75 minutes. England went on to win by one wicket.

Newcastle United lost at home to their great rivals Sunderland 1–9 on December 5, 1908 (a First Division record since equalled). Newcastle, however, went on to win the Championship, while Sunderland finished third.

England follow on — and win. In the first Test of 1894–95, Australia scored a record 586 and England followed on 261 runs behind. They then scored 437, bowled Australia out for 166, and won by ten runs.

Sceptre won four Classics in 1902, the 1,000 and 2,000 Guineas, the Oaks, and the St Leger, and she came fourth in the Derby!

C.B. Fry played in 26 Tests for England between 1895 and 1912, captaining them in six and scoring two hundreds. In 1893, he equalled the world long-jump record. He was also a leading sprinter, he won a soccer cap and played for Southampton in the Cup final, and he played rugby for the Barbarians.

Charlie Buchan

Steve Donoghue

Babe Ruth

Jack Dempsey

Dixie Dean

Paavo Nurmi

Jack Hobbs

Suzanne Lenglen

THE TWENTIES

With World War I over, the 1920s heralded an upsurge in sporting activity. The leading footballers, cricketers, tennis players and boxers drew huge crowds, although the Olympics were still struggling to achieve universal acceptance. The exploits of the Finnish athlete Paavo Nurmi, however, did much to draw world attention to the Games. And American swimmer Johnny Weissmuller was also a fine advertisement for Olympic sport before he transferred his talents to the screen as Tarzan.

The 1920s saw the first Wembley Cup final, and soccer was revolutionized by the development of the 'third-back game' — devised at Arsenal by manager Herbert Chapman and veteran forward Charlie Buchan. Meanwhile Dixie Dean was setting unparalleled goalscoring records. 'Come on Steve' was the cry heard on racecourses up and down the country when Steve Donaghue was in the saddle, and the elegant Jack Hobbs was setting prolific batting records on England's cricket fields.

Suzanne Lenglen continued her reign as Queen of Wimbledon, while her compatriots, the 'Four Musketeers' — Cochet, Borotra, Brugnon and Lacoste — shared the men's tennis laurels with America's 'Big Bill' Tilden. Other outstanding American sporting personalities included Babe Ruth, who revolutionized baseball with his spectacular hitting, Walter Hagen, who brought respectability to professional golf, Bobby Jones, the first golfing idol, and Gene Tunney and Jack Dempsey, who fought two memorable fights.

WORLD EVENTS OF THE TWENTIES ... 'Prohibition' in USA ... Stalin comes to power in the USSR ... General Strike in Britain ... Lindbergh flies Atlantic solo ... Wall Street Crash ... world recession ...

Banned from Henley

Kelly wins Olympic Gold

Double Olympic gold-medallist John B. Kelly, father of Princess Grace.

American sculler John B. Kelly was barred from competing at Henley Royal Regatta in 1920 because his club Vesper had been accused of infringing the amateur rules there 15 years earlier. In his absence, British oarsman Jack Beresford won the coveted Diamond Sculls. They met later that year at Antwerp, in the Olympic final, and after a breathtaking race Kelly won by a

second. Half an hour later he teamed up with his cousin Paul Costello to take the double sculls (a win they repeated in the next Olympics).

Kelly was a superb sculler, unbeatable on his day. In 1919 and 1920 he won 126 consecutive races. He also had another claim to fame — his daughter Grace became a famous film star and later Princess of Monaco.

Against All Odds

US Win Olympic Rugby

Rugby union has always been a very minor sport in the United States and few Americans know what it is. How they won the Olympic title in 1920, beating France 8–0, is one of the mysteries of sporting history, although there were only the two entries.

The rugby final.

Carpentier k.o.'s the 'Kid' in one

Georges Carpentier was a great sporting figure before and after World War I. He dominated light-heavyweight boxing and made some exciting excursions into the heavyweight division. The 'Pride of Paris', he won European Championships at four weights. He was as popular with the ladies as with the male fight fans.

Carpentier earned a crack at the world heavyweight title in 1921 but was battered to defeat by the great Jack Dempsey in four rounds. And although he was never quite the same again, he was more than a match for the best of the British boxers, including that superb fighter Ted 'Kid' Lewis. Lewis stepped up a weight to tackle Carpentier for the world light-heavyweight title, and lost a sensational fight in the first round — Carpentier k.o.'d him as he turned to speak to the referee.

The 'Kid' is counted out.

The First Wembley Final

P.C. on white horse clears the pitch — with a little help from his friends

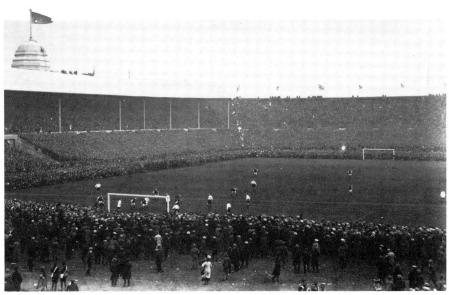

The first Wembley Cup final was a famous milestone in the history of association football. Today, it is every player's dream to play at Wembley, whether he comes from Tottenham or Timbuktu. But on April 28, 1923, that first game very nearly did not take place, and it was a minor miracle that a disaster was averted.

Built for the 1924 Empire Exhibition, Wembley Stadium had been completed only four days before the game. The Football Association, not realizing the amount of interest that would be generated, did not arrange an all-ticket match. In the event, a crowd estimated at a quarter of a million flocked to the ground.

The official attendance was 126,047, but many thousands more (some estimates put it at 50,000) rushed the gates and climbed the walls. The crowd inside overflowed onto the pitch, completely covering it. Thanks, however, to their good sense and the efforts of the police, there was no panic. The start was delayed 40 minutes, but the crowd was eventually pushed back to the touchlines.

In the circumstances, the teams — Bolton and West Ham — played some good football. Corners had to be taken from a standing start and often the ball was kept in play by spectators. It fell to that prince of inside-forwards David Jack to score the first goal, putting Bolton one up after only two minutes, with an opponent struggling to get back onto the pitch after falling among the crowd. Jack Smith clinched it for them in the second half with a thunderbolt shot that rebounded from the mass of bodies pressing against the net. 'It almost hit me on the way out', he said afterwards.

Top to bottom: **Scenes before and during the game — it needed a minor miracle to clear the pitch. P.C. Scorey with his white horse Billy have gone down in soccer folklore, but there were plenty of other policemen on horseback to help him clear the crowds.**

The first Le Mans Grand Prix d'Endurance, to give it its official name, was held on May 26-27, 1923. From the very beginning, it was more than just a motor race. The side-shows, the food and the drink were there to attract the crowds to this 24-hour spectacular. The race was won by a Chenard-Walcker averaging over 92kph, and Duff and Clement set the lap record of 107kph in their 3-litre Bentley. They returned in 1924 to win — and herald the era of the Bentleys.

Left: **The winning Bentley in 1924.**
Below: **Start of the first Le Mans.**

Against All Odds

Cochet comes back from the brink of defeat

The most remarkable turnaround in a major tennis match took place in the men's singles semi-finals at Wimbledon in 1927. American ace 'Big Bill' Tilden was the king of lawn tennis, Wimbledon champion in 1920 and 1921, on his only previous visits. Against the spring-heeled Henri Cochet, he reached a seemingly unassailable position: 6-2, 6-4, 5-1 and 15-all, with the Frenchman serving. Using his immense power, he had brushed aside the artistry of Cochet, and had virtually booked his place in the

final. Then he hit three blistering drives — all out!

Cochet seized his chance, running the 34-year-old American up and down the court. Tilden never gave up, but Cochet took the last three sets.

In the final, Cochet beat his compatriot Jean Borotra, coming back from two sets down for the third match running. Tilden himself was later to make a remarkable comeback, for after two further semi-final defeats he won his third Wimbledon in 1930, at 37.

The Amazing Nurmi

Nurmi (right) holds off Ritola's challenge in the Olympic 5,000m.

Paavo Nurmi was the first 'super-star' of the running track. Stop-watch in hand, he completely disregarded his opponents' tactics. He just ran them into the ground. He was the leading figure of the great band of Finnish athletes who made their country the foremost track and field nation in the 1920s.

Nurmi set 20 individual world records and won nine Olympic gold medals (1920-28), not to mention three silvers. And his extraordinary exhibition of distance running in the 1924 Games has never been surpassed. He remained undefeated in seven races, including heats, over a period of six days, and won five gold medals.

On the first and second days, he won his 5,000m and 1,500m heats. On the third day he won the 1,500m by burning off the opposition after 500m. Then, less than 90 minutes later, he resisted a similar attempt by his 5,000m adversaries to drop him in the first few laps, and gradually left them all behind, except for fellow-countryman Ville Ritola, who bravely pressed him right to the tape.

On the fourth day, Nurmi was first home in the 3,000m team heat, on the fifth he won the 10,000m cross-country — picking up an extra gold medal for the team event — and on the sixth he led Finland to victory in the 3,000m team final (no individual medals were awarded in this event).

Spare a thought for the largely forgotten Ritola, though, who ran in the shadow of his more illustrious team-mate. Few others have exceeded his Olympic haul of five gold and three silver medals.

Memorial to a shot

Most golfers, if asked, will recall a particular shot with pride — an escape shot from rough and trees, perhaps, or a bunker shot laid up to the hole.

One such shot is commemorated with a plaque (pictured right), set in the wall of a bunker at the 17th hole of Royal Lytham and St Annes. The man who made it was the great American golfer Bobby Jones, in the 1926 British Open. With a mashie iron, he hit a sensational recovery some 150m to the green to snatch the title when all had looked lost.

Drama of the Long Count

**Tunney on the canvas for
14 seconds — gets up
to beat Dempsey**

On September 22, 1927, a year after a
ring-rusty Jack Dempsey had lost his
world heavyweight title to Gene
Tunney, 104,943 eager fans flocked to
Soldiers' Field, Chicago, and paid
$2,658,660 to see a return match. What
they got for their money was a contest
that bristled with incident and produced
a sensational moment that has become a
legend in ring history.

Championship fights were ten-
rounders at that time, and for the first six
the pattern was similar to that of their
first fight. Tunney made full use of the
ring, keeping the former champion at
bay with a darting, accurate left to the
face and an occasional right cross. Then,
in the seventh round, Dempsey struck.
Tunney had backed into the ropes and,
reaching them sooner than he
anticipated, was hurled back into
Dempsey's blazing fists, his guard
momentarily down.

In a flash, the 'Mauler' produced one
of the deadliest combinations ever seen
— four magnificent punches to
Tunney's jaw, left and right hooks that
thudded onto the target, causing the
champion's knees to buckle. He sank to
the canvas, his left hand grasping for the
ropes, a dazed look on his handsome
features. Dempsey hovered over him

**Dempsey (left) rushes back for the
'kill', but Tunney has had 14 seconds
to clear his head.**

menacingly, ready to apply the 'kill'.

The referee, in strict accordance with
a recent rule, ordered Dempsey to a
neutral corner. But several seconds
elapsed before he complied — too late,
for the champion had scrambled to his
feet, beating the 'count'. Ringside
observers registered that he had been
down for 14 seconds. He managed to
steer clear of further trouble until
the bell, recovered well in the interval,
then completely out-boxed the tiring
Dempsey in the last three rounds to keep
his title.

Number 60 for the 'Babe'

Looking back, it is strange that there was
not a great deal of fuss the day Babe
Ruth scored his 60th home run of the
season, on September 30, 1927. But he
was only breaking his own record, 59 in
1921, and it was late in the season, with
his club, the New York Yankees, already
having clinched the pennant.

That record, however, soon assumed a
great significance. Of all the baseball
records, it was the most distinguished.
Every American schoolboy knew it,
every great hitter coveted it. It was a
record that stood for 34 years, and even
when it was beaten, with 61 by Roger
Maris in 1961, the new record had an
'asterisk' slapped on it because it was

made in a 162-game season as opposed to
the 154 games of Ruth's season.

Ruth was and is a baseball legend. He
revolutionized the game in the 1920s
with his big hitting, and reigned
supreme for two decades. And his 'magic
60' was a standard of excellence for a
generation.

**Babe Ruth watches his 60th homer
soar over the fence.**

Number '60' for Dixie

Dean (left) heads his 60th League goal, in the dying minutes of the season.

While Babe Ruth was compiling his 60 home runs across the Atlantic, another famous '60' was being completed on the football fields of England. William Ralph 'Dixie' Dean, another sporting legend, scored 60 goals in an English League season. Dean scored his goals for Everton in the 1927–28 season, two years after the change in the offside law

had made goalscoring easier and before tactics had been developed to counteract the new threat. But that should never be allowed to detract from his achievement, for no one has reached even 50 goals since then in the First Division, and today's leading scorers rarely exceed 30.

The build-up to the record during the season and then the climax come straight

out of the pages of schoolboy fiction. The hero was courageous and handsome, and the whole country, dazzled by his skills and great sportsmanship, thrilled to his scoring feats.

Dean scored in each of his first nine games, culminating in five against Manchester United. Fans everywhere began to follow his progress towards the record of 59, set the previous season by George Camsell in Division II. Tensions built up as he beat the club record of 38, then the First Division record of 43. But he needed nine goals in his last three games. He scored two against Villa, and then four in the first half against Burnley, but a pulled thigh muscle left him limping and there were frantic efforts to get him fit for the last game, at home to Arsenal.

He scored two of the three goals he needed in the first half, but time slipped by and there was only five minutes left. Then Everton won a corner. Alec Troup lifted a hanging cross to the far post. And there was Dean, as ever, rising majestically to power his header into the net to a roar that reverberated around Merseyside. It was a moment that has few equals in sporting history. And unless they double the size of the goal, it is a record that will probably never be beaten.

The Wembley Wizards

They said it was Scotland's finest victory over England — the 'Auld Enemy' — since the Battle of Bannockburn, that 5–1 thrashing at Wembley on March 31, 1928. And it has remained so for over half a century. Since then, England have humiliated the Scots by scores of 7–2 and 9–3, but no other clash between the two has had such an impact on football history.

It might seem puzzling to the young that this victory of the team forever known as the 'Wembley Wizards' way back in the twenties has been immortalized. It wasn't that England were a great side at the time or that the fixture had any great significance — the Championship had already been decided, with Wales the winners. The answer lies in the sheer magic of the Scottish football, the artistry of their forwards and half-backs that produced play the like of which, some say, has never been seen since.

On a wet surface, the tiny Scottish attack, with Alec Jackson easily the tallest at 1.70m, swept England aside by playing the pure, classic style of Scottish football — ground passes combined with individual dribbling. Jackson scored a hat-trick, thanks to three perfect crosses floated over from the opposite wing by Alan Morton. Alex James — then a goalscorer with Preston before he became a goalmaker with Arsenal — hit two beauties past the overworked Hufton in the England goal. Other stars were centre-forward Hughie Gallacher, inside-right Jimmy Dunn, and wing-half Jimmy McMullan.

Years later, even the English critics were still raving about Scotland's performance. Sadly, they have never played like it again.

Jimmy McMullan leads Scotland out, followed by Alec Jackson and Hughie Gallacher.

Speedway goes international

It is generally agreed that speedway was born in a small Australian town — West Maitland, in New South Wales — in 1923. Its growth as a major world sport, however, began on February 19, 1928, when the Australians first took their exciting new sport to Britain. That first meeting, at High Beech, in Epping Forest, east of London, made a big splash at the time, and despite one or two crises Britain has become the major world centre for the sport.

A huge crowd turned up to watch this novel, daredevil form of racing, and they weren't disappointed, with thrills and spills aplenty. There were two Australians present to demonstrate the art of 'broadsliding', which had become the accepted way in Australia of taking the sharp bends on the dirt tracks. The sport mushroomed all over the country, and as early as 1929 there were league competitions and individual championships. The old stagers who recall those early days of speedway say they were the most exciting in the history of the sport.

The front page of the Daily Mirror **announces the birth of a new sport in Britain, dirt-track motor-cycling, which later became known as speedway. It is interesting to note (bottom left) that at the same time Malcolm Campbell was breaking the world land speed record.**

The perfect dive

At the 1928 Olympic Games in Amsterdam, Pete Desjardins became the only diver in Olympic history to earn maximum points for a dive. And he did it twice, during the springboard event, which he won easily. He won a second gold medal in the high board, this time by a narrow margin. An American born in Canada, he was known as the 'Little Bronze Statue from Florida'.

Other great moments and exploits of the twenties

Jack Gregory, Australian all-rounder, scored 100 and took 7–69 against England at Melbourne in 1920–21, and at Johannesburg a year later scored a hundred in 70 minutes, the fastest in Test history.

Two enduring 300's. In the 1928 season, A.P. 'Tich' Freeman of Kent and England took 304 wickets (averaging 18.05). In 1928–29, A.F. Kippax (260 not out) and J.E.H. Hooker (62) put on 307 for the tenth wicket for New South Wales against Victoria. Both records were still standing over fifty years later.

Johnny Weissmuller won five Olympic swimming titles, the 100m, 400m, and freestyle relay in 1924, when he also gained a bronze medal in water polo, and the 100m and relay in 1928. He also set 24 world records.

Second All Blacks, led by Cliff Porter, swept through Britain and France on their 1924–25 tour, winning all 30 matches. Known as the 'Invincibles', they scored 721 points to 112.

Steve Donoghue rode a unique hat-trick of Derby winners (1921–23).

Don Bradman

Fred Perry

Sonja Henie

Jesse Owens

Gordon Richards

Alex James

Jim Sullivan

Lionel Van Praag

THE THIRTIES

International sport flourished in the thirties, with the birth of the World Cup and the coming of age of the Olympics. Not that the World Cup received the blessing of the British countries — they were to remain aloof until 1950. England staked a claim to supremacy with home victories over first the Austrian 'Wunderteam' and then Mussolini's Italy, the World Champions. Domestically, Herbert Chapman's Arsenal achieved unprecedented success, inspired by the mercurial Alex James.

In 1936, Nazi Germany cynically mixed sport and politics to stage the most spectacular sports gathering the world had seen, using the Olympics to throw a veil of respectability around their evil regime. Ironically, the 'Master Race' was upstaged by a Negro from Ohio, Jesse Owens, the athlete of the decade.

Nor was it all goodwill and sportsmanship on the playing fields of the Empire — cricket's 'bodyline' controversy led to considerable ill feeling between England and Australia. But England's dubious bowling tactics put only a temporary brake on Don Bradman's unparalleled ability for making runs.

On the racetracks Gordon Richards rode winner after winner, season after season. Other prodigious record-breakers included Sonja Henie, who in 1936 chalked up her tenth consecutive world ice-skating title; Jim Sullivan, rugby league full-back who amassed points by the bucketful; and Sir Malcolm Campbell, fastest man on land and water. Another speed merchant was Lionel Van Praag, first world speedway champion, and Fred Perry's speed around the court won him a hat-trick of Wimbledon championships. And, of course, there was 'Babe' Didrikson, the greatest sportswoman of all time.

'ORLD EVENTS OF THE THE THIRTIES ... invention of jet engine ... Nazis come to power in

rmany ... abdication of Edward VIII ... Spanish Civil War ... first Nylons and Biros ... outbreak of World War II ...

Grand Slam

In the days before big-money golf, the 'Grand Slam' comprised the US and British Amateur and Open championships. The only man to win all four in one year was American Bobby Jones.

Between 1923 and 1929, he had won nine of these major titles, but the British Amateur had eluded him. He finally won it in 1930 at St Andrews, after a struggle. The Open at Hoylake was easier, and he returned to New York for a ticker-tape welcome.

He then won the US Open by two strokes, a margin he owed to his famous 'lily pad' shot, when his ball is said to have skipped three times on the surface of a lake before hopping onto the bank. He won the US Amateur easily to complete the Grand Slam, and then retired — still only 28.

The First World Cup

A stuttering start

Nattily dressed referee John Langenus of Belgium watches the opposing captains greet each other before the first World Cup final, in Montevideo.

The idea of a world soccer championship was as old as FIFA itself, but it was not until 1929 that Uruguay got the go-ahead to stage the first World Cup — in 1930. Because of the distances involved, only three teams travelled from Europe — Belgium, France, and Yugoslavia. The British countries were absent, having withdrawn from FIFA in 1928.

There were 13 entries, seeded into four groups. The refereeing left much to be desired, and the competition was riddled with disputes — more often than not concerning Argentina. They eventually reached the final to play Uruguay, both sides having won their semi-finals 6–1.

In front of a fiercely partizan 100,000 crowd, Uruguay took the lead, but Argentina went in 2–1 up at half-time. In a surprisingly sporting game, however, Uruguay scored three second-half goals without reply to win 4–2.

It was a stuttering start, and there were, of course, Argentinian complaints of one-sided refereeing and Uruguayan brutality. But at least it was a start.

The Magnificent 'Run Machine'

Don Bradman's record-breaking tour

The Australian tour of England in 1930 had gone down in history as 'Bradman's tour'. He scored hundreds in four of the five Tests, including two double centuries and a record 334 at Leeds. His final tally was 974, beating Wally Hammond's record series aggregate of 905, made against Australia in 1928–29. Bradman's Test average in 1930 was 139.14, a mark he was to exceed the following season against the South Africans, when he averaged a mind-bending 201.50.

Bradman had given notice of his remarkable run-getting ability as a 20-year-old when England toured Australia in 1928–29. Although overshadowed by Hammond, he notched two hundreds in his first Test series, for a highly respectable average of 66.85.

A bowler's nightmare, Bradman had extraordinarily fast reflexes. He always seemed to be in the perfect position to play the stroke he wanted. He had all the strokes, as well as a marvellous gift for improvisation, and he placed the ball with uncanny precision. He was rarely subdued for long, and scored his runs at a brisk pace. In his sensational 334 in the third Test, he made a century before lunch and was unbeaten at the end of the day with 309, after passing the previous record of 287 made 27 years earlier by England's R. E. Foster at Sydney.

Bradman sets off for another run during his historic 334 against England.

How's That for Openers!

Record opening partnership by Yorkshire pair

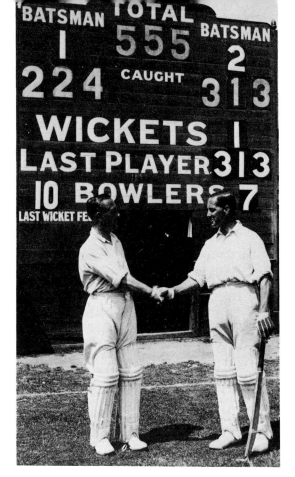

In August 1898, two Yorkshiremen, Jack Brown and John Tunnicliffe, set a cricketing record that was to last for over 30 years. Against Derby, they put on 554 for the first wicket, Brown making 300 and the tall Tunnicliffe — 'Long John of Pudsey' — 243. On the small Chesterfield ground, their stand took only 305 minutes.

In 1932, another Yorkshire pair, Percy Holmes and Herbert Sutcliffe, came out to open against Essex at Leyton on June 15. The following day, when Sutcliffe was bowled for 313, they had reached the magic figure of 555. At first it was thought they had only equalled the record, but a no-ball was found to have been omitted from the score. It took them 450 minutes to break the record on the large Leyton ground. Sutcliffe hit a six and 28 fours, Holmes 19 fours in his 224. The only chance either gave was said to have been a missed catch when Holmes was 3. Over the years, the pair enjoyed a record 69 opening century partnerships for Yorkshire.

Some fifty years later, their partnership still stands as an English record for any wicket, although Walcott and Worrell put on an unbeaten 574 for the fourth wicket for Barbados in 1946 and a year later Hazare and Gul Mahomed made a tremendous fourth-wicket stand of 577 for Baroda.

One-Woman Team

'Babe' wins match on her own

It was a spring afternoon at Dyche Stadium, Evanston, scene of the 1932 US women's national championships and Olympic tryouts. Some 200 girls were taking part, and as each team was announced the squad of a dozen, maybe twenty, athletes would run out to gentle applause from the spectators. The name 'Employers Casualty Company' was announced . . . and a lone girl ran out waving her arms to a deafening roar from the crowd. That girl was Mildred 'Babe' Didrikson.

At high school, Mildred had been a star basketball player, and she went to work for Employers Casualty, an insurance firm, to play in their team. She was soon chosen for the All-American team. She tried her hand at track and field, and won various events in the women's national championships in 1930 and 1931. So in 1932 Employers Casualty sent her as a 'one-woman team'.

She entered eight events, and for 2½ hours was flying all over the place. She won five outright and tied for first in another. The 30 points she amassed was enough to win the team championship. The Illinois Women's AC came second — with a team of 22!

King of land and water

Sir Henry Segrave was the first man to hold both land and water speed records at the same time. A famous sporting figure of the twenties, this son of an Irish father and an American mother had won a place in the Sunbeam team in 1921 through sheer tenacity, and in 1923 won the French Grand Prix — the first British driver to win a GP in a British car. In the late 1920s, still driving a Sunbeam, he set about the land speed record, raising it three times in his 'duel' with Malcolm Campbell to a final 231.44mph (372.47kph) in 1929, in an Irving-Napier, his famous *Golden Arrow*. He was knighted in the same year. Then, in 1930, in his boat *Miss England II*, he broke the water speed record with 98.70mph (158.84kph) on Lake Windermere. He was killed soon afterwards, trying to improve his own record, when his boat struck a log at over 100mph.

Zabala, floppy hat in hand, drags his tired body over the line.

Experience of Youth

The 1932 Olympics at Los Angeles threw up its share of sporting heroes. Among them were two young athletes competing in vastly different events but each making history in his or her own way.

The tiny Argentinian Juan Carlos Zabala probably weighed a lot less than his normal 52kg as he broke the tape at the end of a gruelling marathon. With three other finishers in the stadium at the same time, Zabala forced himself round the track to beat off the challenge of the fresher Sam Ferris of Great Britain, who left his effort too late. There was only 19 seconds between them.

A 20-year-old from Buenos Aires, Zabala was nevertheless already an experienced runner, with the world 30,000m record to his credit as well as a runaway victory in the Kosice marathon. He had led for much of the way, and his courageous finish provided a fitting finale to the track and field programme.

The other 'youngster' to shine at Los Angeles was also an experienced athlete — Babe Didrikson. Restricted by the rules to a maximum of three events, she set new world marks in winning the javelin and the 80m hurdles. In the high jump, however, she suffered a curious disqualification, and had to be content with silver. After a tie with fellow American Jean Shiley at 1.65m, another world record, they both failed at the next height. And although they then both cleared 1.66m in a jump-off, the Babe's effort was ruled illegal. It was a preposterous decision, and it is no wonder that this great athlete later turned to golf.

The 'Babe' about to break the world javelin record in the Olympics.

After Bradman's demolition of the England bowling in 1930, England captain Douglas Jardine got together with fast bowler Harold Larwood to devise a method for curbing this 'run machine' on the 1932–3 tour of Australia. Out of their deliberations came 'leg-theory', or 'bodyline' as it became known. Little did they realize what they were starting. British standards of sportsmanship would be called into question, ill-feeling created between the teams, the England fast bowlers booed on the field by the Australian spectators, and even friendly relations between the two countries threatened.

Leg-theory was nothing new. It entailed bowling at or just outside the leg stump with a predominantly leg field, inviting the batsman to give a catch to the 'leg trap'. This bowling at the body had to be fast and accurate to meet with

McCabe cheered off

In the face of England's bodyline bowling, the Australians produced two great individual innings — the 187 not out by Stan McCabe (seen, above, being applauded off the field) in the first Test, and Bradman's courageous 103 not out that set up Australia's only win, in the second Test.

Controversy

Larwood and Co. terrorize the Aussies, but was it cricket?

success, although on the high-bouncing Australian pitches the hook stroke was fraught with danger.

Larwood was simply devastating. His speed and accuracy were unsurpassed, and he was to take 33 Test wickets on the tour. But the controversy began to develop in the first few matches, in which Larwood, because of an injured toe, did little bowling. Of England's other quick bowlers, Bill Voce and Bill Bowes bowled short and fast at the batsmen, while Gubby Allen — an amateur — shunned the bodyline method for the orthodox attack on the off stump. In the early games, the MCC met with huge success, beating three leading State sides by an innings and restricting Bradman to an average of 17 in six innings.

In the first Test (with Bradman unable to play), England won by 10 wickets despite a marvellous century from McCabe. Larwood took 10 for 124. In the second, a superb hundred by Bradman and some fine spin bowling by Bill O'Reilly (10-129) on a dead

Melbourne wicket levelled the series for Australia.

It was during the third Test, with Woodfull and Oldfield both felled by Larwood, that the cables began to fly between Australia and Lord's. The MCC, somewhat arrogantly, brushed aside the Australian protests, as England went on to win the series 4-1, and it was not until the touring side returned that the full seriousness of the controversy was appreciated.

Eventually, intimidating bowling was banned by law (limiting the number of 'bumpers'). Larwood, one of the truly great bowlers, later settled down in Australia. And Bradman, who had averaged 'only' 56.57 in the bodyline series, was never contained again in Test cricket.

Right: **A batsman's view of Larwood.**
Below: **Don Bradman is caught in England's leg trap, by Gubby Allen off the controversial bowling of Larwood (appealing, half way down the wicket), in the third Test.**

Walsall's Day of Glory

On January 14, 1933, the football world was stunned as the third round FA Cup results produced the scoreline 'Walsall 2 Arsenal 0'. Mighty Arsenal, the most feared side in the land, had been beaten by a run-of-the-mill Third Division side. Arsenal were riding high at the top of the First Division at the time. They had reached at least the sixth round in all but one of the previous seven seasons, including three finals, and were probably the best organized side the game had known.

There were, of course, excuses. Three novices had been drafted into the Arsenal side because of a flu epidemic. The tiny Walsall ground was unfamiliar.

And if Walsall's game was somewhat vigorous, who could blame them for taking advantage of a lenient referee? Arsenal missed chance after chance; Walsall made the most of their few. The name of Walsall became synonymous

Walsall (in striped shirts) upset the mighty Arsenal in the Cup.

with giant-killing, and although there have been comparable upsets since, Arsenal have never lived down that catastrophic day.

Wimbledon thriller

Another turn-up in 1933 came at Wimbledon with the defeat of Ellsworth Vines in the singles final. After the ease of his victory in 1932, he was regarded as invincible. With a cannonball serve and a fearsome forehand drive, he had defeated his opponent, Australian Jack Crawford, for the loss of only six games in the 1932 semi-finals. But Crawford had been practising methods for countering the American's power. And in what turned out to be one of the greatest finals in Wimbledon history, he won by 4–6, 11–9, 6–2, 2–6, 6–4.

Vines (right) congratulates Crawford after their epic final.

'What do you do when you're out of luck?'

Don Bradman's prolific batting dominated cricket in the thirties. In seven Test series, five of them against England, he scored 4,625 runs, averaging over 100, and slammed 19 centuries. He rewrote the record books, with scores of over 300 coming twice in Tests and four times in State cricket, including a record 452 not out for New South Wales.

Nevertheless, regarded by many — including Bradman himself — as his finest knock was an innings he played against Middlesex in 1934. For it came when he was out of form.

Middlesex had been dismissed for 258 by five o'clock on the Saturday, and Bradman came in shortly afterwards when Woodfull was lbw to the second ball of the Australian innings. He played and missed at the first two deliveries, and each time the ball shaved the off-stump. Turning to the veteran

England Test player Patsy Hendren at slip, he asked: 'What does a man do when he's out of luck?' Hendren advised him to 'have a bang'.

And that is precisely what Bradman did. He proceeded to take the Middlesex bowling apart. However defensive the field, Bradman found the gaps. His stroke-play was a joy to watch. With quickness of eye and foot, he dispatched even the good-length balls to the boundary. The excitement began to mount as a hundred before close became a possibility. He needed 25 runs in 12 minutes. The crowd were willing him to his hundred, and tantalizingly he made them wait until the last ball of the day before he stroked a single wide of mid-on to hoist the magic 100 — made in 77 minutes, out of 135. Those privileged to be at Lord's that Saturday evening had witnessed the innings of a master.

Three Great Hat-Tricks

A trio of titles

In the 1930s, Arsenal was the name on every football follower's lips. They captured the imagination of the nation; they were loved by their fans, hated or envied by others, but always respected. Having won the Football League Championship in 1931 and narrowly missed both League and Cup in 1932, they then proceeded to chalk up a hat-trick of titles, only the second club to do so. They owed their success to manager Herbert Chapman, who sadly died at the height of their fame.

Twinkling star of Arsenal's triumphs, Alex James leaves three opponents gasping at his genius.

Drake's Seven

On December 14, 1935, the 70,000 fans at Villa Park witnessed the finest individual scoring feat in First Division history. It is exceedingly rare for a side to score seven away from home in Division I, but Arsenal did it that day, and even more remarkable—Ted Drake scored them all. And he had only eight goal attempts — the other one hit the bar!

200 winners—three seasons running

Until Gordon Richards came along, 200 winners in a season was a rare feat for a jockey. The great Fred Archer had regularly accomplished it in the late 19th century, but since then there had been only one other instance. Even the immensely popular Steve Donoghue was unable to reach 150 in his 10 seasons as champion jockey.

Richards took over from Donoghue both as champion and as the punters' favourite, and by 1932 had won six jockeys' titles. Then in 1933 he passed Archer's record of 246 winners, amassing a total of 259. Also that year, he rode a record 11 consecutive winners. He went on to notch 200 winners in both 1934 and 1935.

Richards continued riding into the 1950s, making some of his early riding feats seem commonplace. But it was in the 1930s that he began to set standards of consistency that might never be surpassed.

Triple Victor

Hungarian table tennis star Victor Barna won all three world titles in 1935 — singles, doubles, and mixed. He had done this treble before, in 1932, but this time he won a fourth gold medal, in Hungary's Swaythling Cup team. It set the seal on a 7-year period in which he won 20 gold medals. Barna's style and athleticism helped rid table tennis of its 'ping-pong' image and elevate it to a world sport.

Victor Barna (right), with the world singles trophy in 1935, is congratulated by runner-up Mike Szabados, his team-mate and partner in six of his world doubles triumphs.

The amazing Jesse Owens

At Ann Arbor, Michigan, on May 25, 1935, one man embarked on an orgy of record-breaking unparalleled in the history of athletics. The scene was Ferry Field, venue of the annual 'Big Ten' inter-university meeting, and the star performer was Jesse Owens, the 'Tan Streak from Ohio State'.

Owens lined up for the 100 yards with a slightly strained back, but the soreness disappeared with the sound of the starter's gun. He streaked away to equal the world record with 9.4 sec. He then trotted casually over to the long jump pit and, with the announcer focusing the crowd's attention on him, unleashed the first ever 8-metre jump, lopping 15cm off the previous record. His 8.13m mark was to stand for 25 years.

His other four records were set in two races — the straight 200yd and 200m in 20.3sec (unbeaten for 14 years) and then the straight 220yd and 200m low hurdles in 22.6sec. Barely 45 minutes had elapsed since the start of the 100yd!

Owens leaps 8.13m (26ft 8¼in), a record that stood for 25 years.

Prince Obolensky's try

The only Russian prince ever to have played rugby for England, Alexander Obolensky scored one of the most memorable tries in rugby history in January 1936 against the touring All Blacks.

Obolensky about to touch down.

Born in Petrograd (now Leningrad) in 1916, Obolensky was brought to England at the time of the Russian Revolution. He was educated at Oxford, and was selected for England a month after winning his rugby Blue. He scored two tries in the match, the first after 25 minutes, but it is for the second that he earned undying fame. Playing on the right wing, he was about 30m out when he received the ball, just before half-time. Coming in from the touchline, he took a pass from his fly-half and cut inside. He weaved his way right across the field, wrong-footing opponent after opponent with his beautiful body swerve before rounding a last desperate tackle to score.

It is still described by many followers as the greatest try scored at Twickenham, and it ensured New Zealand's first ever defeat on English soil.

First 300 mph

Malcolm Campbell first broke the world land speed record in 1924, with 146.16mph (235.22kph), beginning a long tussle with Henry Segrave and others. In all, Campbell broke the record nine times, culminating in his 301.13mph (484.62kph) in 1935, set in his Campbell-Special *Bluebird*.

Sir Malcolm Campbell in *Bluebird*.

The Brown Bomber's Revenge

Louis thrashes Schmeling

Perhaps the most popular boxer there has ever been, Joe Louis was a quiet, reserved man, whose behaviour in and out of the ring was impeccable. It is said that he only ever once fought in anger, and that was in his return fight with German Max Schmeling.

Louis won his first 27 fights, beating two former world heavyweight champions, Primo Carnera and Max Baer. Then he came up against another former champion, Schmeling, who sensationally knocked him out in the 12th round.

But six more wins earned Louis a crack at the title, and he disposed of James J. Braddock in the eighth. A year later, in 1938, he got the fight he wanted — with Schmeling. Louis, a Negro, was fuming about German insults to his race, for dictator Adolf Hitler was using Schmeling to prove the superiority of the Aryan race. Louis set about Schmeling from the bell. With left hooks and right crosses, he had the German down three times and the referee stopped the fight after just 124 seconds.

Louis prepares for the 'kill' as Schmeling hangs onto the ropes.

Perry's Perfection

A former world table tennis champion (1929), Fred Perry transferred his talents to the tennis court and in 1936 became the first man since World War I to win the Wimbledon singles title three years running. He won all his finals in straight sets, culminating in his 6–1, 6–1, 6–0 defeat of German Gottfried Von Cramm in 1936, before turning professional.

Sporting Oddities

The Long Point

In the 1936 Swaythling Cup, the men's world team championship of table tennis, the Romanians were making a farce of the game — and winning all their matches — by 'chiselling', tactics that involved just pushing the ball back and waiting for their opponents to make a mistake. But against Poland they met their match. Alex Ehrlich arrived at the table determined not to attack. The first point of the first game — against Romania's Farcas Paneth — took 2hr 5min before Ehrlich won it with a net cord. The demoralized Romanians went on to lose the rubber 5–0.

Sonja Supreme

In the 1930s, a petite, attractive Norwegian girl reigned supreme as queen of the ice rink. When she retired to take up a successful screen career in 1936, Sonja Henie had just won her tenth successive world skating title and her third successive Olympic gold. With a wide repertoire of spectacular spins and jumps, she did more than anyone to popularize the sport.

Owens' Olympics

Four golds for the 'Tan Streak'

The staging of the 1936 Olympics in Nazi Germany was the first major example of how feeble and misguided sporting bodies, in their anxiety to 'keep politics out of sport', defeat those very aims by woolly thinking. Hitler and Goebbels used the Berlin Games as an instrument of propaganda to dignify the evil philosophy of the Nazi regime. They were the biggest and best Games organized yet. With huge swastikas lining the massive 100,000-seater stadium, the scene resembled one of Hitler's notorious and fanatical youth rallies.

Although the Germans, with a team over 400 strong, won more gold medals even than the Unites States, only five of these came in athletics, all in the throwing events. The Americans dominated track and field, winning 14 titles. And, to the consternation of the Nazi propagandists, it was the black American athletes who shone brightest of all, particularly Jesse Owens, who made his name synonymous with these Games.

Arriving in Berlin as world record-holder in seven events, Owens was the centre of attention. After his first victory, in the 100m, he was mobbed by admirers wherever he went. His duel with local hero Luz Long in the long jump had the crowd enthralled, and Long could not have endeared himself to his Fuehrer by his friendly and sportsmanlike attitude to his ebony adversary. Competing in the long jump immediately after winning his first heat in the 200m, Owens had fouled his first two qualifying attempts. He had one more chance, and it was his rival Long who advised him to adjust his run-up. He soared over the qualifying mark, which was almost a metre below his world record. In the competition proper, Owens led Long by only 3cm after four jumps, and then Long equalled Owens' best effort. But with his last two jumps, Owens took himself well out of the range of the gallant German, and his final leap of 8.06m (26ft 5¼in) was to stand as an Olympic record until 1960.

Owens went on to win two more gold medals, taking the 200m with ease and anchoring the US team to a world record in the sprint relay. It was the eighth world record for the 'Tan Streak from Ohio State', and crowned one of the greatest performances in Olympic history.

New Zealand's First

In what was rapidly becoming the Blue Riband of the track, the greatest field to date lined up in Berlin for the 1,500m final. It included all the 1932 medallists — champion Luigi Beccali of Italy, runner-up Jerry Cornes of Britain, and Phil Edwards of Canada — plus world mile record-holder Glenn Cunningham of the United States, and Jack Lovelock, a New Zealander based in England and former mile record-holder. The only star missing was the injured British champion Sydney Wooderson.

Lovelock was a runner who believed he could reach his peak only once or twice a year. He had prepared all season for this race, and he planned his tactics to perfection. Cunningham and the Swede Eric Ny cut out the pace, while the crinkly-haired, black-vested New Zealander moved inexorably through the field. Cunningham tried to drop the field on the third lap, but Lovelock went with him, and with 300m to go he struck — earlier than expected. There was no answer, and he opened up a gap of some ten metres. He hit the tape in 3min 47.8sec, a second inside the world record. Cunningham also beat the old mark, and the first five smashed the old Olympic record. It was New Zealand's first Olympic gold medal in athletics.

Speed King Campbell

Having put the world land speed record out of reach of mere mortals for the time being, Sir Malcolm Campbell was at a loose end in the mid-1930s. He noticed, however, that the water speed record was in American hands. Intensely patriotic, he set about winning it back for Britain. He did so in 1937 on Lake Maggiore (pictured right) with a speed of 208kph (130mph).

Hutton's marathon

Don Bradman (right) is the first to congratulate Hutton on beating his Test record.

Len Hutton's record-breaking effort against Australia in the 'timeless Test' at the Oval in 1938 generated fever-pitch excitement throughout the country. As the 22-year-old Yorkshireman passed one batting milestone after another, the whole nation thrilled to his gargantuan feat of concentration, determination, and faultless technique, and when he struck the four that took him past Bradman's record 334, the ground erupted. Hutton made 364 in 13hr 20min. The rest of the match was an anticlimax.

Cup Final Drama

Mutch scores penalty winner in extra time

The 1938 FA Cup Final at Wembley between Preston and Huddersfield had been a dreary, disappointing affair. Little of note had occurred and the match went into extra time. Then, suddenly, in the very last minute there was drama. George Mutch, Preston's

Scottish international inside-left, made a determined run through the middle. Just as he got through to Huddersfield's penalty area, Alf Young came across to tackle. He appeared to get the ball away, but Mutch went down and the referee gave a penalty. It was the first penalty-

The last kick of the 1938 Cup final — Mutch's spot-kick goes in off the cross-bar to give Preston victory.

kick awarded in a Wembley final. Mutch himself took it, and scored — with the last kick of the match.

Other great moments and exploits of the thirties

Marjorie Gestring of the United States, at 13, became the youngest ever individual Olympic champion when she won the 1936 springboard diving event in Berlin.

Richard Bergmann, 16-year-old table tennis ace, gave notice of things to come when he won all three of his matches in the final of the 1936 Swaythling Cup to give Austria a 5–4 victory over Romania.

Bob Tisdall of Ireland scored a dramatic victory in the 1932 Olympic 400m hurdles, after only a handful of races at that distance. He broke the world record, but it was not allowed because he knocked over a hurdle.

Gene Sarazan, US and British Open Golf champion in 1932, looked like finishing second in the 1935 US Masters until he holed his second at the 15th from 210 metres. It gave him an 'albatross' (three under par), and he went on to force a play-off and win the following day.

Jim Sullivan, Welsh-born full-back who played rugby league for Wigan, kicked 204 goals in the 1933–34 season, a record that stood for nearly 40 years.

Donald Budge of the United States became the first player to complete the 'Grand Slam' of the four major tennis titles in one year, in 1938.

Don Bradman and Bill Ponsford scored 451 for Australia's second wicket in the fifth Test against England at the Oval in 1934 — a Test record for any wicket that still stands.

Henry Cotton carded a record-equalling 283 at Sandwich to win the Open Golf Championship and break an American ten-year monopoly in the event.

Benny Lynch of Scotland, in what many regard as the greatest fight between two British-born boxers, scored a sensational 13th-round knock-out over unbeaten 19-year-old Englishman Peter Kane in Glasgow to retain his world flyweight title.

Joe Louis

David Freeman

Joe Davis

Denis Compton

Fanny Blankers-Koen

Jack Kramer

Reg Harris

Sydney Wooderson

THE FORTIES

The outbreak of World War II in September 1939 virtually put a stop to international sport. On the domestic front, wartime sport was improvised, more as entertainment than as serious competition. In England, little Aldershot, for example, as a military centre, were able to call upon the services of some of the country's top footballers. At various times they fielded such stars as Tommy Lawton, Joe Mercer, and Stan Cullis.

In some countries, sport continued for a time as usual. Before they joined the war, the United States thrilled to the batting feats of baseball hero Joe DiMaggio, and Joe Louis successfully defended his world heavyweight title 13 times in the early 1940s. In Sweden, those great athletes Gundar Haegg and Arne Andersson were rewriting the middle-distance record books — Haegg alone set 15 world records. Britain's Sydney Wooderson, a most unlikely looking athlete, was coming to the end of his career, but made a wonderful comeback by winning the European 5,000 metres in 1946. England stepped in to host the first post-war Olympics, and Dutch athlete Fanny Blankers-Koen won four gold medals.

Champions who continued to reign after the war included Joe Louis, Joe Davis (snooker), David Freeman (badminton), and Don Bradman (cricket), while the sportsmen who made their mark in the late 1940s included Denis Compton (cricket and football), Jack Kramer (tennis), and Reg Harris (cycling).

WORLD EVENTS OF THE FORTIES ...Japanese attack Pearl Harbor... Allies invade Europe...

rmany surrenders ...atomic bombs dropped on Japan...formation of UN...first supersonic flight...

Hit Man

Ask anyone but an American who Joe DiMaggio was and they will tell you, if they remember the name, that he was a baseball player who married sex symbol of the screen, Marilyn Monroe. Ask an American, especially one who was around in the spring and summer of 1941, and he will tell you that Joe DiMaggio was the New York Yankees' centre-fielder who hit safely in a record 56 consecutive games.

A quiet, modest man, the eighth of nine children of an Italian-born crab fisherman in Martinez, California, DiMaggio became a national hero. In December of that year the American people would be drawn suddenly into the world conflict by the Japanese attack on Pearl Harbor. But in the early months, Americans from all walks of life would listen to the latest news reports to hear the announcement: '. . . and in sports Joe DiMaggio today extended his hitting streak . . .'

First he beat the Yankee record of 29, then the National League record of 33. When he finally beat the major league record of 44, he did it in style with a home run. The magic number of 56 has never been approached.

The Dashing Dynamos

The Dynamos were the sensational Moscow side that flashed all too briefly onto the soccer scene in 1945 with a short tour of Britain before Russian football disappeared from international view again for several years. They attracted 271,000 to their four games, the crowd breaking down the gates at Stamford Bridge to see them draw 3–3 with Chelsea. They cut a dashing style, on the field and around the country, thrashing Cardiff 10–1, beating a reinforced Arsenal 4–3 (in the fog with, at their own insistence, a Russian referee!), and holding Glasgow Rangers 2–2. Then they were gone.

Below: **Dynamo's keeper 'Tiger' Khomich saves at Stamford Bridge.**

Mr Tennis

Seeded No. 1 and hot favourite, Jack Kramer predictably won the Wimbledon singles title in 1947. He lost only 37 games in his seven matches, the most one-sided Wimbledon triumph in the men's event. It was perhaps ironic for someone born in Las Vegas that Kramer created the concept of 'percentage tennis' — playing the shot that gives you the most chance of success as opposed to 'gambling' on hitting spectacular winners. Kramer turned professional later that year, and proceeded, first as player-promoter and then as promoter, to revolutionize the game and pave the way for 'open' tennis.

Left: **Kramer's Wimbledon triumph.**

44

A Season of Seasons

The 'Terrible Twins' run riot in 1947

South Africa suffer as (left) Compton sweeps a ball to the boundary and (right) acknowledges the cheers for a double century.

The 'Terrible Twins' they called them, as Denis Compton and Bill Edrich ravaged the best of England's bowlers up and down the country and tore the touring South Africans apart for good measure. Never in the history of the game have two batsmen from the same county so dominated the batting averages, as Middlesex won the Championship for the first time in over a quarter of a century. In all first class matches, Compton scored 3,816 runs (average 90.85) and Edrich 3,539 (80.43), both beating Tom Hayward's record of 3,518 made in 1906. And Compton's 18 hundreds beat the 16 of Jack Hobbs, made in 1925. Batting at numbers three and four for both county and country, the pair shared in no fewer than seven partnerships of over 200 during the season, including one of 370 in the second Test against South Africa. Compton scored six of his hundreds against South Africa, including four in Tests, in which he amassed 753 runs for an average of 94.12.

But mere statistics do not tell the story of Denis Compton. They are incidental to his joy in playing cricket and the immense pleasure and thrills he gave those who watched. A natural at both cricket and football, he endeared himself to the crowds with his cavalier spirit and unorthodox — often cheeky — play. He played wartime soccer for England, but his cricket and two 'dodgy' knees curtailed his career. Even so, he went on to earn League and Cup winners medals

with Arsenal, as an outside-left with a deadly left foot and, of course, a penchant for the unusual.

Compton was 29 in 1947 and, despite constant knee trouble, continued to play cricket for another ten years. His greatest innings, perhaps, was his 145 not out against the Australians at Old Trafford in 1948, after being knocked out by a Lindwall special early on.

The 'Terrible Twins', Edrich (left) and Compton, take the field to continue another prolific and entertaining partnership.

Good Evans!

Denis Compton shared a most remarkable stand with wicket-keeper Godfrey Evans for England against Australia at Adelaide in February 1948. Having scored 147 in the first innings, Compton was rapidly running out of partners in the second when the normally ebullient Evans arrived at the wicket. He stayed there for a record 95 minutes before he scored his first run! They were eventually unbeaten, adding 85 in 2¼ hours. Compton scored 103, Evans 10, and the match was saved.

'Ferocious Fred' v 'Gutsy Gus'

Mills beats Lesnevich to win world title

Mills has Lesnevich on the canvas during their second fight.

Britain's Freddie Mills and America's Gus Lesnevich were fighters who gave their all. Their two epic battles in the late forties left them both bloodied, battered, and bruised, yet they became and remained firm friends out of the ring.

Both fights took place in London. In 1946, Lesnevich crossed the Atlantic to defend his world light-heavyweight crown at Harringay Arena, and knocked the ring-rusty Mills off his feet in the second. Barely conscious, Mills fought back magnificently before finally succumbing in the tenth. The return at the White City in 1948 was a different story. This time, Mills kept his guard up. He dropped the champion for two counts of nine in the tenth and went on to win the decision and with it the world title.

Boy wins man's event

Those spectators who stayed on at Wembley till near midnight on August 6, 1948, witnessed one of the outstanding feats of the modern Olympics. They saw a boy, just out of school, become, at 17 years 9 months, the youngest ever competitor to win an Olympic athletics title. But what was so remarkable about Bob Mathias's performance is that he won his gold in a 'man's event' — the decathlon.

Harrison Dillard (No. 69) wins the 1948 Olympic 100m final. Britons Alastair McCorquodale (36) and McDonald Bailey (35) were 4th and 6th.

Mathias's discus throw gave him a lead he never lost.

Hurdler wins Olympic sprint

In 1948, Harrison Dillard was indisputably the best high-hurdler in the world. In April, he set a new 120yd hurdles record, and by June had run up a string of 82 consecutive wins. Then, suddenly, his whole world fell about his ears — he stumbled in the US Olympic trials and failed to make the team. So he qualified for the 100 metres dash instead.

As American third string, he won his first and second round heats at Wembley, and then his semi-final. The other Americans, Barney Ewell and Mel Patton, were still favourites when they lined up for the final. But Dillard showed in front almost from the start and held off Ewell at the tape.

Dillard went on to win a second gold in the United States sprint relay team, and in 1952 he duly won his Olympic hurdles title, and collected his fourth gold in the relay again. His final Olympic tally was 12 races, 12 wins.

46

The Flying Dutchwoman

Fanny Blankers-Koen (right) just edges out Britain's Maureen Gardner in the final of the 80m hurdles. Both clocked a world-record 11.2sec.

Bursting like a sudden ray of sunshine onto the drab, wet Olympic scene at Wembley in 1948, Fanny Blankers-Koen won an unprecedented four gold medals for a woman at one Games. She soon became known as the 'Flying Dutchwoman', setting the crowd alight with her explosive start, and rattling off win after win on the Wembley track.

Coming to the Games with seven world records — including the high and long jumps, which she did not enter — she was encouraged by her husband and coach, Jan Blankers. She beat British girls into second place in her three individual events — Dorothy Manley in the 100 metres, Maureen Gardner in the 80 metres hurdles, and Audrey Williamson in the 200 metres. But still the crowd loved her. Her crowning triumph came in the 4×100 metres relay. Collecting the baton metres down in fourth place, she surged up the straight and just got up to beat Australia's Joyce King at the tape.

The 30-year-old housewife stamped her character and personality on the London Olympics and left an indelible memory with those lucky enough to be there and watch her perform.

Other great moments and exploits of the forties

Don Bradman retired in 1948 after Australia's tour of England. Needing only 4 in his last Test innings for an average of 100, he was bowled for a duck. Nevertheless, his average of 99.94 (over 52 Tests) puts him in a league of his own.

Manchester United won the FA Cup in 1948, playing all six matches against First Division sides.

Everton Weekes scored a record five consecutive Test hundreds for West Indies, the first against England in 1948 and the rest against India in 1948–49.

John Cobb, British speed merchant, became the first man to reach 600kph on land. In 1947 he pushed his twin-engined Railton-Mobil to 634.4kph (394.2mph), beating his own record set eight years earlier.

Cornelius Warmerdam of the United States revolutionized pole vaulting in the early 1940s. Using a bamboo pole, he was a decade ahead of his time in technique, and none of his contemporaries could get near him. He made the first 15-foot vault in 1940, and took the world record to 4.77m (15ft 7¾in) in 1942, a mark that stood for 15 years.

Record partnership of **Holmes** and **Sutcliffe** was beaten twice in the 1940s, first by Frank Worrell (255 not) and Clyde Walcott (314 not), who put on 574 for the 4th wicket for Barbados against Trinidad (1945–46), and then by Vijay Hazare (288) and Gul Mahomed (319), who compiled a 577 4th-wicket partnership for Baroda against Holkar (1946–47), a record for any wicket still standing in the 1980s.

Gundar Haegg of Sweden ran a mile in 4min 1.3sec at Malmö in 1945, a record that was to prove extremely difficult to better.

Emil Zatopek

Lester Piggott

Cliff Morgan

Maureen Connolly

Ferenc Puskas

Stanley Matthews

Peter Thomson

Stirling Moss

THE FIFTIES

As the world gradually returned to normal after the traumas of World War II, sport began to flourish again. The USSR brought their athletes out from behind the 'Iron Curtain' and made an immediate impression on international competition, especially in the Olympics, where they began to dominate the gymnastics and the field events in particular. Germany — soon to be split into East and West — and then Japan returned to the sporting fold.

A popular choice as sportsman of the decade must be Czech athlete Emil Zatopek, who produced some unforgettable performances in the Olympics and took his world record tally to 18 at distances from 5,000m to 30,000m. Another great sportsman, Stanley Matthews, continued his remarkable footballing career, which he climaxed in the 'Matthews final' at Wembley. Hungarian star Ferenc Puskas also set Wembley alight, and the late fifties saw the birth of Pelé's incomparable genius. Lester Piggott's was another precocious talent to emerge in the fifties, while the exciting Maureen Connolly took Wimbledon by storm.

The outstanding individual feat of the 1950s was perhaps Jim Laker's 19 wickets in a Test, while the prize for consistent excellence must go to golfer Peter Thomson, who won four British Opens in five years. Other stars who stamped their personalities on their sports include Rocky Marciano in boxing, Juan Fangio and Stirling Moss in motor racing, Alfredo di Stefano and the tragic Duncan Edwards in soccer, and Cliff Morgan in rugby.

WORLD EVENTS OF THE FIFTIES ...Korean War...first ascent of Everest...hydrogen

bomb...Suez crisis...Hungarian uprising...Common Market founded...Sputnik launched...

England's Humiliation

It happened at Belo Horizonte — a name that sends shudders down the spine of any English football fan over the age of 40. For that was where, during the finals of the 1950 World Cup, England suffered the most humiliating defeat in their history — at the hands of the United States!

A handful of part-timers, the Americans were not given a chance in Brazil. England had won 23 of their 30 post-war internationals. And despite the absence of Stanley Matthews, the presence of Finney, Mannion, Mortensen, and Wright was surely enough to guarantee them a flood of goals.

But they never came — not one. It was one of those days when nothing went right. Four times England hit the woodwork, a header was cleared from a position seemingly over the line, and on other days they might have been awarded two penalties. Then the Americans scored, from their only real chance. It was a bumpy pitch, and England suffered from a lack of preparation — but there really was no excuse for losing to the United States.

Larry Gaetjens scores — it's the United States 1 England 0!

World Record Gate

There was to be no final for the 1950 World Cup. The four group winners met in a final pool. Fortunately, the last match turned out to be the decider, and a world record gate of just under 200,000 crammed into Brazil's Maracana Stadium to see the host country take on Uruguay. Brazil, needing only a draw, took the lead just after the interval. But Uruguay netted twice in the second half to win their second World Cup.

'Calypso Kids'

In the summer of 1950, two West Indian spin bowlers, each with only two first class matches to his name when he left the Caribbean, so bemused the English batsmen that the West Indies gained their first Test victories in England and won the series 3–1. Their exploits became almost legendary, and calypso bands sang the praises of 'Those pals of mine, Ramadhin and Valentine'.

They were an unlikely looking pair — Sonny Ramadhin, who bowled in his cap, and the bespectacled Alf Valentine.

A right-arm off-spinner, Ramadhin could bowl all day, and he baffled the world's best batsmen with the one that turned from leg. Valentine was a left-arm spinner, who used subtlety of flight and prodigious spin to wheedle out his victims. He could also bowl all day.

Both only 20, they bowled several marathon stints in that four-Test series. In the second Test Valentine bowled 116 overs, Ramadhin 115. Valentine finished up with 33 wickets, Ramadhin 26 — at little more than 20 runs apiece.

The Turpin-Robinson Return

Last desperate effort from Sugar Ray

Turpin lies stunned in the tenth as Robinson looms over him.

Tennis 'cure' makes a champion

The history of sport is full of stories of champions who have reached their goal despite terrible handicaps. Some of them triumph *because* of adversity. One such champion was American tennis player Doris Hart. A badly injured kneecap as a child threatened amputation, but loving attention from her mother pulled her through. At nine, however, she was operated on for a hernia. It was after this, to give her exercise, that her brother began to teach her tennis. She never looked back. She became a perfect stylist, and her 35 major titles included the Wimbledon singles crown in 1951.

The worst ever start

The scene was Headingly, in June 1952, during the first Test of the Indian tour. India had just started their second innings, only 41 behind England. Then suddenly the scoreboard read 0 runs for 4 wickets. The crowd were stunned to silence. In just 14 balls, England had virtually won the match. Freddie Trueman had claimed three wickets (and was on a hat-trick) and Alec Bedser one. It was the worst start to an innings in Test history. Trueman was denied his hat-trick, but India never recovered.

Randolph Turpin was world middleweight champion for just 64 days. One of the finest boxers produced in Britain in the post-war period, he had no little boxing skill, but it was his powerful punching that made him such a force in the ring. He had taken the world title from no less a man than Sugar Ray Robinson, regarded not only as, pound for pound, the best boxer around, but also one of the all-time 'greats'.

Fortunate, perhaps, to have taken on Robinson after a whistle-stop tour of Europe in which the champion had fought six fights in five countries in only 41 days, Turpin made the most of his chance. He staggered the boxing world by outpointing Robinson in a thrilling fight at Earls Court, London.

Turpin immediately became a national hero. The first Briton to wear the world middleweight crown since Bob Fitzsimmons in the 1890s, he was fêted up and down the country. Crowds flocked to his training quarters in North Wales. The pressure could not have helped his preparation for the return — a return that contractually had to be held within 64 days.

Exactly 64 days later, on September 12, 1951, the two fighters faced each other again at the New York Polo Grounds, in front of 61,370 fans, a record for a non-heavyweight bout. It was a fitter, sharper Robinson now that Turpin had to contend with. But he still gave as good as he got, and in what has been described as the 'fight of the century' he looked to have Robinson beaten by the tenth round. Behind on points and with his face streaming blood from his cut left eyebrow, the former champion knew he would not be allowed to come out for another round. In desperation, he sprang at Turpin, catching him with right hooks to heart and chin. Turpin keeled over, but rose at the count of eight, only to run into a fusillade of blows rained in at him from all angles. The referee had to intervene, even though there was only eight seconds to the end of the round. Robinson had achieved one of the most dramatic recoveries in ring history.

Zatopek drives for the tape past the fallen Chataway.

Zatopek! Zatopek! Zatopek!

'Zatopek! Zatopek! Zatopek!' was the chant as the popular Czech pounded relentlessly round the track. With an agonized look on his face as if fighting considerable pain, he would nevertheless grind his opponents into the dust as he set record after record in the early fifties and won gold medals galore in both Olympic and European competition.

Emil Zatopek was not only a national hero, but was loved and admired wherever he ran. Regarded by many as the world's greatest ever middle- and long-distance runner, he had pace, boundless stamina, guile, judgement, determination, and his own special brand of aggressiveness on the track that stamped him as the true champion.

Of all his dauntless deeds on the track, his exploits at the Helsinki Olympics in 1952 stand out. He retained his 10,000m title with little difficulty — in fact, he was unbeaten over that distance in 38 races from 1948 to 1954 — beating Frenchman Alain Mimoun by 16 seconds. But four days later, having strolled through his 5,000m heat, he faced a real battle in the final. It turned out to be an Olympic classic. At the bell, there were only four left in contention, with Zatopek lying third and the stout-hearted Chris Chataway tracking him. With 300m to go, Chataway swept into the lead, past the German Herbert Schade. Zatopek would need all his track-craft and guts now. Elbows out and grimacing head rolling, he took Mimoun with him as he powered past Chataway and the German. Dramatically, as he was beaten, Chataway tripped on the kerb and fell. Zatopek went remorse-lessly away from the others. They could not catch him, but this time he had only four-fifths of a second to spare over the Frenchman at the tape.

Then Zatopek announced he was going for the marathon. He had never run a full competitive marathon before, but his grinding training schedules had prepared him well. No one doubted his ability, but could he recover only three days after such a gruelling 5,000m?

In the event he ran all the experienced marathon men into the ground. And when he entered the Olympic Stadium, the Finns rose to him as if they were welcoming one of their own track immortals. They gave him what has been described as the greatest sustained ovation ever accorded an athlete. For Emil Zatopek had accomplished the 'impossible treble'.

51

Rocky Batters His Way to Title

The ringcraft of the ageing Joe Walcott was not enough to stop the relentless Rocky Marciano taking his world title.

On September 23, 1952, Arnold Raymond Cream stepped into the ring to defend his world heavyweight title against Rocco Francis Marchigiano. And the Cream–Marchigiano fight turned out to be one of the classic heavyweight bouts of all time — Jersey Joe Walcott v Rocky Marciano.

At 37, Walcott had been the oldest fighter to become heavyweight champion when he knocked out Ezzard Charles the previous year. Marciano, at 28, was also a late developer. Many thought he had been overmatched, and they were nodding knowingly when Walcott put him down with a sizzling left-hook in the opening round. But they, and the champion, were staggered to see Marciano get up at two and renew his two-fisted attack to Walcott's head.

It was a tremendous see-saw fight, with the champion ahead in the 13th, when suddenly Marciano exploded a right to the jaw, one of the hardest single punches ever seen in the ring. It was the end of Walcott.

There was a return, but Walcott lasted less than a round. Rocky went on to another five title defences, and retired in 1956, undefeated.

Angelica repels Oriental invasion

The Japanese arrived on the table-tennis scene in the early 1950s, and revolutionized the game with their sponge bats and all-out attacking penholder style. Both their men and their women began to mop up most of the world honours. But one player to stop them in their tracks was Romania's Angelica Rozeanu, the 'queen of table tennis'.

Fast and graceful, with a superb all-round game, she won 17 gold medals in world events. She won six consecutive singles titles (1950–56), and despite the all-conquering Japanese led Romania to five team titles (Corbillon Cup) between 1950 and 1956. Her finest year was 1953, when in addition to the singles crown and a Corbillon Cup gold, she won the ladies' and mixed doubles events, too.

Catches win Matches

If ever the old cricket adage 'Catches win matches' rang true it was in South Africa's famous victory over the Australians in the second Test of the 1952–53 tour. First, Jack Cheetham parried a sizzler for Hugh Tayfield to turn and catch the ball full length. Then Cheetham and Jackie McGlew made 'impossible' catches. Finally Russell Endean topped them all by leaping to pluck a Miller 'six' out of the sky on the boundary fence. South Africa went on to win the match . . . but not without the help of a brilliant 162 not out from Endean.

The Matthews Final

Matthews torments a Bolton defender (above) and is chaired by team-mates (below) with his precious medal proudly displayed.

Stanley Matthews was 38 when Blackpool reached the FA Cup final in 1953. It appeared to be his last chance of a winners medal. He had joined Blackpool from Stoke in 1947, already a footballing legend renowned for his right-wing artistry and his sportsmanship. Twice since then Blackpool had reached Wembley, but each time he had to be satisfied with a runners-up medal. And when Blackpool found themselves 3–1 down to Bolton in 1953 with only twenty minutes to go, it looked as if this last chance had slipped by.

What happened next was unfortunate for Bolton, who were depleted by injuries, but it was an emotional time for the whole nation, who were willing Matthews to get his coveted medal. And he didn't let them down. He proceeded to tear the Bolton defence apart with a display of all his guile and wizardry, swerving and feinting, turning his man this way and that, threading his way to the bye-line as he had done a thousand times before. The keeper fumbled his cross, and Stanley Mortensen scrambled the ball over the line. With minutes to go, Mortensen hammered a free-kick in for his personal hat-trick: 3–3.

There were only seconds left, and Matthews had the ball again. He took the ball up to the left-back, feinted to go inside but as usual beat his man on the outside and made for the line. He was in the penalty box. The fans were pinching themselves to make sure it was not a dream. He cut the ball back unerringly to the feet of Perry, who swept it into the net. Matthews had his medal at last.

Hats Off to Sir Gordon

Gordon Richards was the Stanley Matthews of the turf. Admired and respected universally, a genius at his craft, he had been top jockey now for as long as most people could remember. In 1953 he was heading for his 26th championship in 29 seasons and approaching a career tally of 4,800 winners. A dozen times he had ridden over 200 winners in a season, and he had 13 'classic' wins to his name.

But, like Matthews, one thing had eluded him, the most famous prize of all. He had never ridden the Derby winner.

His mount in 1953 was Pinza, one of the favourites. The news of his knighthood was announced just before the race. He took Pinza to a four-length victory. There has never been a more popular winner.

Above: **The finish of the 1953 Derby, with Sir Gordon Richards and Pinza well ahead of the field.** *Left:* **It's hats off to the newly knighted Sir Gordon, on a Derby winner at last.**

Below: **Looks of mutual admiration between Drobny (left) and Patty after their epic contest.**

The Drobny–Patty Marathon

The two men came onto Wimbledon's Centre Court at about five o'clock for their third-round match in the 1953 championships — Jaroslav Drobny, the exiled Czech, and American Budge Patty. The left-handed Drobny's power of stroke gave him the first set 8–6. There were no tiebreakers in those days, and so little was there between the two players it was clear that the match was going to be a long one. It was.

The mobile Patty took the marathon second set 18–16 and the third 6–3. With both men suffering from tiredness and cramp, Drobny saved three match points before taking the fourth set 8–6. And he saved three more before, in the gathering gloom, he triumphed 12–10 in the decider — after 93 games and 4hr 23min on court.

54

Barnacle Bailey

Bailey reaches his 50 with a four off Johnston in the final Test. Last out with 64, he never offered a chance in his marathon innings.

England regained the Ashes from Australia in 1953, winning the series 1–0 with four drawn. But the drawn matches were packed with drama, none more so than the second Test, at Lord's, where England were saved by an epic backs-to-the-wall stand between Trevor Bailey and Willie Watson.

Bailey was a fine all-rounder — an intelligent fast-medium bowler, a brilliant fielder, and a batsman whose defensive qualities had become a nationwide joke. Never was his defiant batting more valuable to England than in the last Test, when his stubborn 64 in 225 minutes was the springboard for England's victory. Bailey's statistics — only 222 runs and 8 wickets in the series — obscure his contribution to England's triumph. Ask any of his opponents!

The Magnificent Magyars

November 25, 1953, marked the end of an era for English football. When the result 'England 3 Hungary 6' was flashed around the country, there were many who at first refused to believe it. It was unthinkable that an unheralded continental side could win at Wembley.

England's first home defeat by foreign opposition (apart from Ireland's largely forgotten 2–0 win at Goodison Park four years earlier) was achieved by perhaps the finest national side the world has seen. The speedy, fluent, confident Hungarians gave a display that would have shattered any team. England, ill-prepared, and possibly over-confident after so many invincible years, were not in the same class. Not that they played badly. Their first two goals were brilliantly taken. But the 'Magyars' were so superior in almost every aspect of the game that the margin must have been greater had they not slackened off in the last half-hour, after building a 6–2 lead.

The typically insular Englishman knew little or nothing about the Hungarians, yet they had a phenomenal record — it was 22 games and 3½ years since they had been beaten, and in over 50 matches since the war they had averaged four goals a game.

From the first minute of the match, when Nandor Hidegkuti slashed a rising 20-metre shot into the England net, the Hungarians delivered a lesson — a lesson in ball control, in teamwork, in tactics, and in finishing. They tore England's fine defence to shreds. They shrugged off a 13th-minute equalizer with a devastating onslaught on the England goal. They scored three times in a seven-minute spell. The middle one, from their captain, Ferenc Puskas, is still spoken of in awe today. Running on to a

near-post cross, he had his opposite number Billy Wright tackling thin air as he rolled the ball back with the sole of his boot and rifled it into the net in one beautiful, flowing movement.

England never recovered. Hidegkuti completed a hat-trick, and the tactic of playing him as a deep-lying centre-forward completely baffled the England defence. They had still not solved their problems the following year when Hungary again humiliated them — 7–1 in Budapest.

Puskas (10) celebrates his famous goal, with England's defence in tatters.

First Four-Minute Mile

Roger Bannister captures the 'Holy Grail' of athletics

The world record in the mile — the Blue Riband of the track — had taken a hammering during the war years from Swedes Haegg and Andersson. But previous to that it had been reduced only four times in the 1930s and once in the 1920s. By 1954, Haegg's 1945 mark of 4min 1.3sec had stood for so long that it, and the 4-minute barrier, began to assume almost divine dimensions. It had become the 'Holy Grail' of athletics.

Then three athletes, from diverse parts of the world, began to approach Haegg's time. The race was on — on tracks thousands of miles apart.

When Roger Gilbert Bannister and his training companions Chris Brasher and Chris Chataway plotted their tactics for a mile race in Oxford, they knew that this might be Bannister's last chance. Bannister, fourth in the 1952 Olympic 1,500m, had done a time of 4min 2sec. But Australia's John Landy had half a dozen similar times to his credit, and the young American Wes Santee had clocked 4min 2.4sec.

The afternoon of the race was wet and blustery. Luckily, however, soon after six, as the runners went to their marks, the wind dropped. Brasher led for 2½ laps, with Bannister trailing him and lapping at 57.7sec and 60.6sec. When Brasher flagged, Chataway took over, dragging Bannister through the ¾ mile in 3min 0.7sec. Now was the chance for the fast-finishing Bannister — but did he have enough in reserve? With 230 metres to go, he summoned himself for his supreme effort and sped past Chataway. Surging round the last bend and up the final straight with his long stride, he was stretched to the limit. As he broke the tape, he was close to exhaustion.

He had broken the world record, no doubt at all, but what about the magic four minutes? The 1,200 spectators who had just been shouting their lungs out were hushed, waiting. Then came the announcement, which seemed to take almost as long as the race, as Norris McWhirter tantalizingly recited Bannister's credentials and the list of records he had just smashed, from track to world, until he came to '. . . the time is THREE . . .' The rest of the announcement was lost as the crowd went wild.

Mile of the Century

Just 46 days after Bannister's epic run at Oxford, John Landy clocked 3min 57.9sec, lopping 1.5sec off Bannister's time. The scene was set for the 'mile of the century' in Vancouver in August. The race was the final of the Commonwealth Games mile. The front-running Landy took an early lead which he stretched to 15yd after two laps. But Bannister gradually pulled it back, and pounced on the last bend, just as Landy looked over his other shoulder. Bannister held on to win by 5yd, and both men broke four minutes again.

Landy looks round as Bannister passes him with 70yd to go.

Opposite page: **The magic moment, as Bannister breaks the tape at Oxford, on May 6, 1954.** *This page, from top to bottom:* **Brasher (44) led for over two laps before Chataway (42) took over. Coach Franz Stampfl (left) helps to support the exhausted hero after the race.**

57

The gallant Jim Peters staggers and even crawls towards the finish.

Her Greatest Victory

After her athletics triumphs of the early 1930s, Mildred 'Babe' Didrikson turned to golf. And, of course, she became the greatest woman player in the world. As Mrs Zaharias, she won tournament after tournament in the 1940s and early 1950s. But perhaps her greatest victory was to come back in 1954 to win her third US Open, after an operation for cancer the previous year.

Triumph for the Red Fox

Chris Chataway, who had helped both Bannister and Landy to their mile records in 1954, enjoyed his own moment of glory at London's White City later that year. The barrel-chested, flame-haired Chataway — the 'Red Fox' — was an immensely popular character on British tracks, with a reputation for courage and for getting by with the minimum of training. He was up against the new 'Iron Man' of athletics, the Russian Vladimir Kuts. Kuts had run away from the great Zatopek in the European 5,000m, and although Chataway also beat the ageing Czech, he couldn't catch Kuts. The Russian would kill off his opponents with a succession of searing bursts. But that night in October, Chataway clung to his heels throughout, and thrust past him on the line to set a new world 5,000m record.

Chataway catches Kuts on the line.

The Peters Marathon

Having reduced the marathon 'world's best' four times in the previous two years, Britain's Jim Peters came to the Commonwealth Games in August 1954 as hot favourite. He looked like confirming expectations when he entered the stadium three miles ahead of the next runner, but it was soon apparent that he was in trouble. Dehydrated in the 75° heat of the Vancouver afternoon, he had lost all sense of balance and was staggering from side to side. It was a repeat of the 'Dorando marathon' in the 1908 Olympics. Like a legless drunk, he tottered on. Heroically and instinctively he refused to give up. A dozen times he picked himself up. The few yards he covered took about ten minutes, and he was finally carried off 200 yards from the line. He never ran again.

'Typhoon' Tyson

Above: **The 'Typhoon' in action.**
Left: **Johnson is caught by Evans, and Tyson has wrapped up the second Test for England.**

Nearly all the drama of England fast-bowler Frank Tyson's brief career was packed into a couple of months. It was on the 1954–55 tour of Australia, where he helped to make cricket history by inflicting on the Australians one of the severest reverses they have ever suffered in a home series. There were other major factors, notably the performance of his fast-bowling partner Brian Statham. But it was Tyson's ferocious speed — he soon earned the nickname 'Typhoon' — that devastated the Australian batting. In the second Test he took 10–130, including a match-winning 6–85 in the second innings to level the series. In the third Test his 7–27 in the second innings was another match-winning performance. He finished up with 28 wickets, averaging 20.83 despite a 1–160 stint in the first Test.

Morgan Inspires Lions

Welsh wizard turns the tide

Springbok flanker Basie Van Wyk is too late to prevent Cliff Morgan from scoring the try that sparked a memorable victory for the Lions.

Against All Odds

A record 95,000 at Ellis Park, Johannesburg, saw the British Lions beat South Africa 23–22 in the first Test of the 1955 tour. They witnessed a see-saw thriller in which the lead changed back and forth and which reached a nerve-racking finale when the Springboks just missed a conversion.

The Lions played most of the second half with only 14 men. They were three points down when they lost one of their forwards, but that magical Welsh fly-half Cliff Morgan inspired their recovery with one of his finest tries. Taking the ball at speed from scrum-half Dickie Jeeps, he jinked through the Springbok defence with a diagonal run across their '25'. Arcing excitingly towards the goal line, he crossed it to touch down under the posts. The tide had turned. The Lions forgot their handicap, and produced a brilliant spell of attacking which gave them victory.

Relentless Rocky Mauls Moore

When world light-heavyweight champion Archie Moore earned himself a crack at the heavyweight title, he was 42 — ten years older than the champion, Rocky Marciano. The two met at the Yankee Stadium, New York, on September 21, 1955.

Instead of attacking the counter-punching Moore in his usual bull-like way, Marciano decided to let the older man make the running. This puzzled even the ring-wise Moore, but not for long. In the second round, he got Marciano to miss with a right, and immediately stepped in to smash the champion in the mouth with what he described as one of the best right-hands of his life. Down went Marciano, for only the second time in his career. Then, to the amazement of the onlookers — and especially Moore — he struggled up at 'five'. In the next few rounds, a desperate Moore threw caution to the winds and went all out for a knock-out. He knew he could not last the distance with this human tank. But Marciano took everything Moore threw at him. If anything, he seemed to get stronger with each round. It was his turn now to go after the older man. Relentlessly he moved in with his short-punching, crab-like style. Moore went down in the sixth, but came up fighting. The end came in the ninth. Moore could barely see as the champion hit him with a terrifying combination, which finally put him out.

It was Marciano who retired after the fight. 'Old Moore', to everyone's amazement, continued to rule the light-heavyweight roost for another six years.

Marciano connects with a right that makes Moore's hair stand on end.

Open Hat-Trick

Australian golfer Peter Thomson never took to the lucrative American circuit, but he was the dominant figure at home and in Britain for a long period from the mid-fifties.

In all, he won five British Opens, a tally unsurpassed in modern times, and he is best remembered for his hat-trick of victories from 1954 to 1956. His triumphs at Royal Birkdale, St Andrews, and Hoylake were a tribute to his consistency, and he was the first to accomplish this feat since 1882.

Thomson won again in 1958 after coming second in 1957. When the leading Americans began again to contest the event, he surprised them all by winning his fifth in 1965.

Winter perfection

Toni Sailer was an artist on skis, the darling of the crowds. A plumber from the Austrian Tyrol, he was 20 when he competed in the 1956 Winter Olympics at Cortina. And he made history there by winning all three ski events, the first man to do so. Yet more significant than the three gold medals was the margin of his victories.

First came the giant slalom. Starting 18th in deteriorating snow conditions, he finished an astonishing 6.2sec ahead of the next man. Then, in the special slalom, he produced the fastest two runs to give him exactly 4sec over the runner-up. Finally, in his favourite event, the downhill, he overcame dreadful conditions that brought down 73 of the 90 starters to win by 3.5sec. The three victories also earned him the world combined title.

In a sport where gold medals are usually won by fractions of a second, his winning margins were astonishing. He completely outclassed his contemporaries as no other ski racer before.

Mystery of Devon Loch

Queen Mother's horse has National 'won' but takes 'phantom jump'

No one will ever be able to say for certain why Devon Loch suddenly spreadeagled himself on the run-in to the winning-post in the 1956 Grand National. There are several theories, many of them plausible, but who knows what goes on inside a horse's head?

If ever a horse deserved to win the National, it was the Queen Mother's big brown gelding Devon Loch. Trained by Peter Cazalet and ridden by Dick Francis, Devon Loch had given his jockey a marvellous ride. Francis was to describe later how for the first time in a National he had found it necessary to hold his horse back, such was the reserve of power he felt under him, while the other leaders were being hard-ridden. With barely an anxious moment during the two gruelling circuits of Aintree, Devon Loch had jumped superbly and had taken the last fence with ease, well ahead of the rest of the field. Often in the National, a tiring horse is caught on the long run-in, but Devon Loch was sweeping confidently towards the post, lengthening his lead with every stride. The race was in his pocket now, and a great roar went up from the crowd, anticipating a Royal victory.

Then suddenly, without any warning, it happened. Devon Loch took off, as if to jump a fence, and in a split second was spread inelegantly on the turf. Francis was still in the saddle, and there was a moment when the crowd, hearts in their mouths, thought he might recover. But it was not to be. There was no way he could get Devon Loch going again, and he reluctantly dismounted as Dave Dick took ESB past him for a hollow victory.

No sooner was the race over than the theories began to flow — a 'phantom jump' (there was a water jump alongside the run-in), cramp, a heart attack, or perhaps a sudden reaction to the deafening volume of noise from the crowd? It will always remain a mystery.

Top and below: **Frames from the BBC film of the 1956 Grand National show how Devon Loch, striding purposefully towards the winning-post only fifty metres away, suddenly 'takes off' and spreadeagles himself on the track. He is upright again as ESB passes him, but Dick Francis dismounts and (right) walks disconsolately past the post.**

Laker's Test

Surrey spinner skittles Aussies twice

Surrey off-spinner Jim Laker was proving a thorn in the flesh of the Australians in 1956. Earlier in the season he had taken 10–88 in an innings for his county against the tourists, a rare achievement. Now, at close of play on the second day of the fourth Test at Old Trafford, he had them reeling again, and had done enough to write himself into the record books — as the first English bowler to take nine wickets in a Test innings against Australia. Four days later, on July 31, he was to ensure that he would never be written out of them, with a performance straight out of the pages of schoolboy fiction.

But to begin at the beginning of this historic Test: Laker had been run out for three in an England first innings total of 459, and by tea on that second day had dismissed Colin McDonald and seen his spinner-in-crime Tony Lock account for Jim Burke. Australia were 62–2. Half an hour after tea, they were 84 all out. Laker had claimed all eight wickets, seven of them in 22 balls. His figures of 9–37 were the best in a Test innings for 60 years.

Then, as ever at Manchester, rain intruded as Australia, having followed on, struggled in their second innings, and play was protracted into the last day. Laker had already had Burke snapped up by Lock, and Neil Harvey caught by Colin Cowdrey. But the square-shouldered McDonald was proving a stumbling-block.

By now the pitch had dried out and was beginning to turn again. Laker made the ball lift and bite, and with catchers of the calibre of Lock, Cowdrey, and Alan Oakman, the Australians had little margin for error. Lock himself, fiercely competitive, was wheeling away at the opposite end, turning the ball prodigiously the other way with his left-arm spin. But it was Laker who slowly whittled the Australian wickets away. Oakman took three catches. Miller, Mackay, and Archer all failed to score. McDonald finally perished in the leg trap. Lock got into the act, but only to catch Lindwall. Laker now had nine wickets to his name, with still one to fall.

Lock, bursting for a wicket after more than 50 overs, could do no more than beat the bat. Then Maddocks, shuffling in front of an off-break, was leg before to give Laker figures of 51.2 overs, 23 maidens, 53 runs, 10 wickets, and a match bag of 19 for 90 — a record for any first-class match, let alone a Test. For once it seemed totally irrelevant that England had retained the Ashes.

Laker appeals and Maddocks is out lbw. Not only have England retained the Ashes, but Laker has bagged a record 10 wickets in a Test innings and a record 19 wickets in any first-class match.

Ribot's Last Race

Enrico Camici, Ribot's jockey in all his races, takes the colt to his second consecutive 'Arc', a convincing win over the world's best.

Italian colt Ribot compiled a perfect record — 16 wins in 16 starts. But it was not until his last race that it was fully appreciated how great a horse he was. As a foal, Ribot had been nicknamed 'il piccolo', the little one, and because of his size had not been entered in the principal Italian Classics. But he developed into a powerful colt, and concluded his three-year-old career with a solid win in the Prix de l'Arc de Triomphe. The next year he came to England and won the rich King George VI and Queen Elizabeth Stakes by five lengths, albeit from a substandard field. But his second 'Arc' was won against the best horses from Europe and America, by a convincing six lengths. It is not surprising that Ribot became the world's outstanding Classic sire.

Iron-man Kuts is Uncatchable

Vladimir Kuts took over from the great Zatopek as 'king' of the middle-distance runners in the mid-1950s. Although not as versatile as the record-breaking Czech, he was perhaps the finest front runner of all time. This was never better demonstrated than in the 1956 Olympics, when he destroyed the world's best with his lung-bursting breaks and won two gold medals. Only Britain's Gordon Pirie stayed with him in the 10,000m, until he finally cracked with four laps to go and finished well down. Pirie managed a silver in the 5,000m — but was 11 seconds behind the relentless Russian. Kuts started running late, but for a few years he was uncatchable.

Kuts begins to pull away from three great British runners in the 5,000m, Gordon Pirie (189), Derek Ibbotson (188), and Chris Chataway.

Connolly in action at Melbourne.
Note his withered left arm.

Determination

It was years and years of sheer determination and courage that enabled Harold Connolly to triumph over the severest of handicaps and become a world-class athlete. He had suffered a broken arm at birth, which left it withered. He broke it again four times before he was 15, and when he was fully grown his left arm was 10cm shorter than the right. The son of a footballer, he was determined to succeed at sport, and tried various events before he took up hammer-throwing at 22.

He came to the 1956 Olympic Games at Melbourne as world record holder, having just deprived Russian Mikhail Krivonosov of his world mark. The two fought a ding-dong battle, which Connolly won by a mere 16cm.

It's a new feeling for the exultant Brasher as he breaks the tape.

Fangio's Greatest Race

Fangio hurls his Maserati over the finishing line for a famous victory.

When he lined up in pole position for the 1957 German Grand Prix, Juan Manuel Fangio had already won three of the four GPs that year. There was a snag at the Nürburgring, however, for his Maserati would need a rear tyre change.

Alongside Fangio on the front line of the starting grid were the Ferraris of Mike Hawthorn and Peter Collins. With a breathtaking exhibition of driving over the tortuous 23km circuit, the Argentinian built up a lead of over 30 seconds before he made his pit stop after 12 of the 22 laps. Unaccountably the stop took nearly a minute, and Fangio began to lose more ground because of a heavier tank. Soon the leeway was 48 seconds. Thinking they had the race in the bag, the Ferrari pits signalled 'steady'. That's when Fangio started to go flat out. On the 15th lap he took 12 seconds off the unsuspecting Ferraris, and lap after lap he closed on them, until a furious 20th lap took him within three seconds. First he took Collins — twice — then Hawthorn, and on the last lap increased his lead to 3.6sec. And in winning his greatest race, Fangio also clinched his fifth World Drivers Championship.

Gold from nowhere

While his two friends Bannister and Chataway were breaking records and winning titles, Chris Brasher was plodding along in the background, compensating for his lack of natural ability with a fierce determination. It was Brasher, remember, who made the early pace for the first four-minute mile. He never won a national title, nor won a major event of any kind — that is, until Melbourne in 1956. He was only Britain's third string in the 3,000m steeplechase, but he ran the race of his life. Bursting into the lead with some 300m to go, he shattered the opposition to win by 15m.

Then he had to survive a sensational disqualification, which was rescinded only after a nerve-racking wait of nearly three hours. But Brasher got his gold, a medal conjured up out of nowhere. Britain had many athletes in the postwar years whose expectations of Olympic titles were much higher, yet Brasher was the first British athlete to win an individual Olympic gold medal for 24 years.

64

Dublin's Golden Mile

Herb Elliott takes a crowd through the 4-minute barrier

During his relatively short international running career (1957–60), Herb Elliott was unbeaten and unbeatable. Over that period, he ran 46 races over a mile or 1,500m, and was rarely bothered in any of them. He would usually make his break for the tape with a lap and a half to go, and no one in the world could keep up with this sustained burst.

Until Elliott came along, a four-minute mile was a newsworthy achievement. The tall Australian, with the help of his pioneering coach Percy Cerutty, made it commonplace. And one night in Dublin he pulled four other runners through the magic barrier in what was truly a 'golden mile'.

Lining up with Elliott at Santry Stadium on August 6, 1958, was a field that included Olympic 1,500m champion Ron Delany of Ireland, two other Australians, Merv Lincoln and world 3-mile record-holder Alby Thomas, and New Zealander Murray Halberg, the Commonwealth Games 3 miles champion.

Thomas set the pace — 56.0sec for the first lap, 1min 58.0sec for the half mile. Then Elliott took over, full of running and anxious to beat the mile record. Elliott did not expect anyone to come with him, least of all Lincoln, a man who had for so long run in his shadow. In desperation, Lincoln was trying new tactics. He passed Elliott and led until the bell, reached in 2min 59.0sec. Then Elliott 'changed gear' and there was no stopping him. He surged away, opening up a huge gap, eventually to win by 12yd. His time of 3min 54.5sec lopped a massive 2.7sec off the world record. Lincoln also broke the old world mark, and Delany, Halberg, and Thomas all finished in well under four minutes.

Ibbotson

Who was the first man to run a mile in four minutes? Beware, it's a trick question. The answer is not Roger Bannister, but Derek Ibbotson, who in 1958 recorded exactly 4min 0.0sec for the distance.

This, however, was not Ibbotson's only claim to fame. For a year earlier, this versatile Yorkshireman set London's White City alight when he pulverized an international field to set a world mile record of 3min 57.2sec. Sadly, he never recaptured that form.

From 'fall' guy to champion

When 17-year-old New Zealander Barry Briggs arrived in England in 1952 to ride for Wimbledon, he made an immediate name for himself for the number of times he fell off. Senior riders thought him so dangerous they tried to have him banned.

But Briggs curbed his initial impetuosity to ride for New Zealand in 1953, and make his World Speedway Championship debut a year later. It was not long before he was challenging the best, and in 1957 he won the world title.

It was a dramatic victory for the young New Zealander, for in clinching the title at Wembley he had to beat the Swedish world champion Ove Fundin twice. Having surprisingly lost a point in an early heat, Briggs beat Fundin in heat 12 and they both finished on 14 points after their five rides. The Swede gated first in the run-off, but Briggs forced his way through on the second lap. Fundin fell trying to get back, and Briggs cruised to the first of his four titles.

Briggs with the 1957 world trophy.

Fontaine is chaired off by team-mates after his four goals against West Germany in the last match.

Frenchman hits 13

The 1958 World Cup is remembered chiefly for the exploits of the Brazilians, especially the young Pelé. Another hero of that tournament was Just Fontaine of France.

In the group matches, he scored three, two, and one, and then two more in the quarter-final. France finally met their match in the semi-finals, but Fontaine's goal was the first scored against Brazil in the tournament. And Fontaine still was not finished, for he scored another four in the third-place match to bring his final tally to 13 — still a record for a single World Cup.

Pelé's World Debut

Arms aloft, the young Pelé acclaims a brilliant, impertinent goal for Brazil in the 1958 World Cup final.

Capped at 16, in Brazil's World Cup squad at 17, Pelé now had a world platform on which to exhibit his precocious footballing skills. It was his deflected goal that had finally knocked out the gallant Welsh side in the quarter-finals, and his second-half hat-trick had devastated France in the semi-finals.

In the final, against host country Sweden, the youngster was lining up alongside such illustrious names as Didi, Vava, and Garrincha, and he soon showed he was not overawed in this company with a brilliant, swerving 18-metre shot that struck the inside of the post. The match was being beamed to millions of homes in Europe, and Pelé really served notice of his greatness with Brazil's third goal. Standing in the penalty box a few minutes after half-time, he called for a long ball from Nilton Santos, and, despite being hemmed in by opponents, stopped it on his thigh, flicked it up over his head and over that of the defender behind him, spun round, and volleyed it past a startled keeper. As if that were not enough, he scored with a header to give Brazil a famous 5–2 victory. Pelé had arrived on the world scene.

Arms aloft, the young Pelé acclaims a brilliant, impertinent goal for Brazil in the 1958 World Cup final.

Billy's 100th Cap

Billy Wright was the first footballer from any country to win 100 international caps. He was the epitome of the true sportsman — loyal, consistent, and always giving a hundred percent. A fine defender and a captain who led by example, he took Wolves, his only club, to their triumphs of the fifties. In all, he played 105 games for England, first as a hard-working wing-half (59 games) and from 1954 as a centre-half (46), his last 90 games as captain.

Wright's 100th international was his last appearance at Wembley, and appropriately enough it was against Scotland, against whom he had made his debut in the 'victory' international of 1946. England won 1–0, and it was an emotional match for the fans, who stood to show their appreciation as Wright was carried shoulder-high at the finish.

Ron Clayton (left) and Don Howe chair their captain, Billy Wright, off the field at the end of his 100th international at Wembley in 1959.

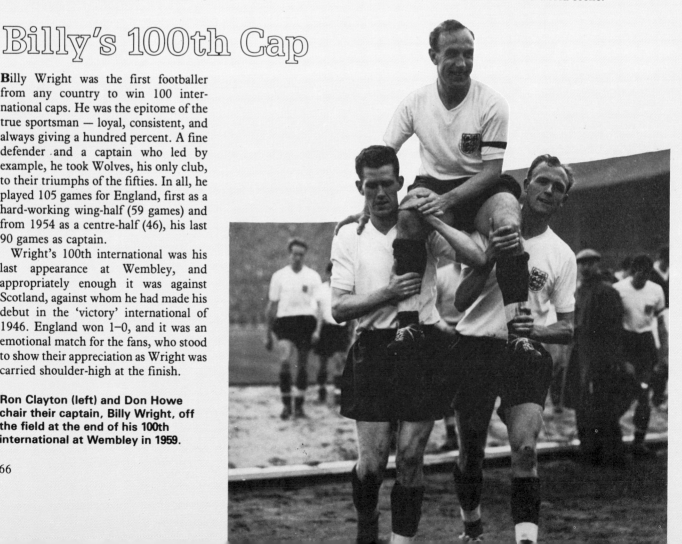

Thor's Hammer

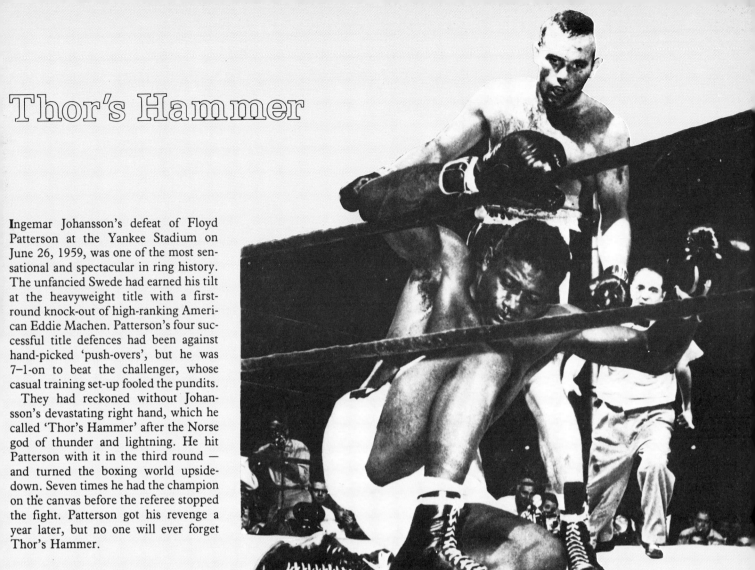

Ingemar Johansson's defeat of Floyd Patterson at the Yankee Stadium on June 26, 1959, was one of the most sensational and spectacular in ring history. The unfancied Swede had earned his tilt at the heavyweight title with a first-round knock-out of high-ranking American Eddie Machen. Patterson's four successful title defences had been against hand-picked 'push-overs', but he was 7–1-on to beat the challenger, whose casual training set-up fooled the pundits.

They had reckoned without Johansson's devastating right hand, which he called 'Thor's Hammer' after the Norse god of thunder and lightning. He hit Patterson with it in the third round — and turned the boxing world upside-down. Seven times he had the champion on the canvas before the referee stopped the fight. Patterson got his revenge a year later, but no one will ever forget Thor's Hammer.

Patterson struggles vainly to shake off the effects of 'Thor's Hammer'.

Other great moments and exploits of the fifties

Marjorie Jackson, Australian sprinter, won the 100m and 200m Olympic titles in 1952. She broke or equalled ten individual world records in the early 1950s, and won seven Commonwealth golds before she retired at 22.

Shirley De la Hunty (née Strickland) won the 1952 and 1956 80m hurdles, taking her Olympic medal tally to a record seven for a woman athlete.

Maureen Connolly became the first woman to achieve the 'grand slam' of tennis, the four major singles titles in one year (1953). She won all three Wimbledons she entered (1952–54)

Joe Davis made snooker's first ever maximum break of 147 in 1955.

Gary Sobers, the great West Indian all-rounder, hit a Test record 365 not out against Pakistan in 1958.

Gary Player of South Africa became, at 23, the youngest winner this century of the British Open Golf Championship (1959).

Ben Hogan, crack American golfer, made a remarkable recovery from a car smash in 1949 to win the 1950 US Open. In 1953, at 40, he won all five tournaments he entered, including the US Open, Masters, and British Open, an unprecedented feat.

Geoff Duke won six world motor-cycling championships in the 1950s, including a hat-trick in the 500cc (1953–55).

Richard Bergmann won his second Swaythling Cup gold medal in 1953 with England, 17 years after his first success as the 16-year-old star of the Austrian team.

Ronnie Moore of New Zealand became the youngest world speedway champion when he won the title in 1954 at 21.

Pat McCormick, American diver, won the two women's events at both the 1952 and the 1956 Olympics.

George Best

Gary Sobers

Cassius Clay

Ron Clarke

Palmer & Player

Billie Jean King

Jim Clark

Rod Laver

THE SIXTIES

In the 1960s, the Olympics got bigger and bigger, and the 1968 Games in Mexico City were clouded by political controversies and arguments about the high altitude, which gave competitors from 'high' countries an advantage in stamina events. Not that the emerging African nations needed it — athletes such as Abebe Bikila and Kip Keino had already established their worth. But Mexico City's thin air virtually denied Australia's record-breaking Ron Clarke his last chance of a gold medal.

British football had a tremendous boost with England's World Cup triumph in 1966, followed by the European successes of Celtic and Manchester United. In Bobby Charlton, Denis Law, and George Best, United boasted three of the world's finest and most exciting players.

Tennis went 'open' in 1968, and Rod Laver returned to renew the domination of the game he relinquished when he turned pro in the early sixties. And Billie Jean King began to establish herself as an 'all-time great' with a hat-trick of Wimbledon titles in the late sixties.

In golf, the sixties are remembered for the 'Big Three' — Arnold Palmer, Jack Nicklaus, and Gary Player. The sixties also saw West Indian captain Gary Sobers establish himself as arguably the greatest all-round cricketer of all, and racing driver Jim Clark win a record number of grands prix before he was tragically killed in a crash. And there arrived on the scene the most flamboyant character in sporting history, 'Big Mouth' himself, Cassius Clay, later to be known as Muhammad Ali.

WORLD EVENTS OF THE SIXTIES   ...Berlin Wall...assassination of President Kennedy...

Yuri Gagarin first man in space...The Beatles...Russian invasion of Czechoslovakia...first men on the moo

Soccer Perfection

10-goal treat at Hampden

Di Stefano, in the all-white of Real Madrid, puts them ahead.

Considered by most pundits as the finest club match in football history, the 1960 European Cup final had everything. As well as the goals, there was the sheer artistry of the football, the dazzling teamwork and sparkling individual displays.

Real Madrid, who had won all four of the previous European Cups, had built a reputation as a team that went for goals. Their play revolved around the Argentinian 'maestro' Alfredo di Stefano. Now they had the veteran Hungarian Ferenc Puskas, who found a new lease of life in Spain. Their opponents, Eintracht Frankfurt, were no pushovers, as they demonstrated in the semi-finals with six goals against Glasgow Rangers in each leg.

And it was the German side who went ahead after 18 minutes. But as usual it was Di Stefano who took complete control of the match, demoralizing the Germans with two goals in three minutes. Puskas then took the stage, and with that left foot of his almost making

the ball 'talk' he scored four, before Di Stefano wrapped it up with a majestic seventh goal that gave him his hat-trick. Refusing to be completely outplayed, Eintracht scored two more, so the final

result was 7–3.

As the heroes of Madrid paraded the Cup at the end, the largely Scottish crowd of some 127,000 remained to give them a magnificent ovation.

Barefoot in the Dark

In the 1960 Olympics, the marathon was splendidly organized to take the runners back along the torch-lit Appian Way at night. What a spectacle it was for the crowd lining this historic thoroughfare — and what a surprise as they saw in the lead an almost unheard of Ethiopian, Abebe Bikila, running in bare feet.

Abebe continued on his effortless way to win Ethiopia's first ever gold medal. He finished 25 seconds ahead of the next man, and his time of just over 2¼ hours was a new world's best.

But Abebe's triumph was more than an isolated victory, sensational as it may have been, for it ushered in a whole new era of running, as athletically backward African nations began to develop their rich natural talents. Abebe himself went on to become the first man to retain the Olympic marathon title, when he left the field trailing by over four minutes in Tokyo only six weeks after having his

appendix out! Encouraged and perhaps inspired by Abebe's breakthrough, middle- and long-distance athletes from such countries as Kenya, Tanzania, and Tunisia became a force in world athletics.

Ethiopia continued the Abebe tradition with athletes such as Mamo Wolde, who won the 1968 Olympic marathon, when Abebe himself was forced to retire in great pain from an incipient fracture to a bone in his leg. Tragically, Abebe was involved in a near-fatal car crash in 1969, which left him wheelchair-bound, and he died four years later. But those bare feet of his left an indelible impression on the world of long-distance running.

Barefoot Ethiopian 'unknown' Abebe Bikila begins to draw away from Morocco's Rhadi Ben Abdesselem along the torch-lit Appian Way.

69

A Minor Miracle

Wilma Rudolph wins the 1960 Olympic 100 metres with gazelle-like grace from Britain's Dorothy Hyman.

It was a minor miracle that Wilma Rudolph ever ran at all. A crippled child of a poor black family in Tennessee, she had just about everything going against her. One of 19 children, she contracted double pneumonia and scarlet fever at four, losing the use of her left leg. She was seven before she could walk again, with the help of special shoes. Yet somehow she survived her misfortunes and grew up to be a tall, athletic teenager with a love of sports. And at 16, she won an Olympic bronze medal with the American team in the sprint relay at the 1956 Melbourne Games.

But that is not the end of the story. For four years later, in Rome, she emerged as one of the outstanding personalities of the Games, captivating the crowds with her grace and charm. Slender — at 1.80m, she weighed only 60kg — and powerful, she won both sprints by impressive margins and took a third gold medal in the relay.

The next year, she set a new 100m world record, and retired before the next Olympics. But her successes, and her remarkable triumph over adversity, inspired many young American Negro girls to take up the sport, and one of them, Wyomia Tyus, went on to win the Olympic 100m in both 1964 and 1968.

Fox's Final   . . . but he's not the man of the match

The 1960 Rugby League Challenge Cup final at Wembley is remembered largely for Wakefield Trinity's comprehensive 38–5 thrashing of Hull and for Neil Fox's contribution — seven goals and two tries, a record 20 points. Yet it was not Fox who won the Lance Todd trophy, awarded to the outstanding player of the match. This went to Hull hooker Tommy Harris, who defied concussion to return to the field after twice being carried off.

Hull had been hit with a crippling list of injuries before the game, and such was Wakefield's superiority they would have crushed any opponents. Only heroic Hull defence kept the score down, and this was typified by the bravery of Harris.

Fox, however, had only another two years to wait before he was awarded the coveted Lance Todd trophy. In Trinity's 12–6 victory over Huddersfield, both sides scored two tries, and it was Fox's three dropped goals that made the difference, the first time such an individual defeat had been performed at Wembley.

The following year Fox won his third Cup medal. But there was a strange sequel to the Fox success story in 1968, when Neil missed the final through injury and his brother Don took over the

goalkicking duties, landed two beauties, and, although Trinity were behind, won the Lance Todd award, voted for before the end of the game. A sensational last-ditch try then gave Trinity a chance for victory. But, with the last kick of the match, Fox missed a straightforward conversion from in front of the posts — a sweet and sour ending to a dramatic and gripping match.

Neil Fox touches down for a try in the 1960 final at Wembley.

The Tied Test

With the advent of one-day cricket, exciting finishes are not uncommon, but there has been nothing to match the drama of the first Test of the 1960–61 West Indies Australian tour.

West Indies arrived in Australia as underdogs, but an effortless hundred from Gary Sobers helped them to a first innings of 453. Australia topped this by 52, thanks largely to Norman O'Neill's 181, and fine bowling from Alan Davidson left the Australians needing a comfortable 233 runs to win.

Then an inspired piece of fast-bowling by Wes Hall had Australia reeling at 92 for 6. But Richie Benaud and Davidson averted the crisis with a stand of 134. When Davidson was run out, only 7 runs were required. Wally Grout took a single off Sobers, and prepared to face the last eight-ball over from Hall, with 6 needed to win and three wickets left.

Off the first ball, Grout scampered a leg-bye. But Benaud was caught behind off the next. Ian Meckiff blocked the third ball, and scrambled a hazardous bye off the fourth: 4 needed off 4 balls. Grout then slogged the fifth ball, and

Hall made a complete mess of the catch and conceded a single: 3 needed off 3 balls. Meckiff cracked the sixth ball into the outfield. They galloped two, and turned about for a third. But Conrad Hunte's throw was perfect and Grout was run out: 2 balls left, scores level, and the last pair in. Hall powered up to the wicket. Lindsay Kline steered the ball

It's a tie! The West Indians are jubilant as Meckiff fails to beat Joe Solomon's throw.

wide of square leg, but Solomon pounced on the ball, picked up and threw down the stumps with Meckiff's bat only inches from the crease. Australia were all out. Test cricket had seen its first tie.

Double Champions

In the first season of the Football League, Preston won both League and Cup. Eight years later, in 1896–97, Aston Villa also achieved the 'double'. After this, the double began to be elusive. Competition in England got tougher and tougher, with more big clubs capable of winning trophies. Several came close to the coveted double, none more so than the 'Busby Babes' in 1957. This thrilling young Manchester United side, under the guidance of Matt Busby, had strolled off with the Championship, but had the Cup snatched from them by a cruel injury to their keeper at Wembley.

There seemed to be a jinx on sides going for the double, and the pundits were saying it was impossible in the modern English game.

Then along came Spurs, in 1960–61.

With a mixture of shrewd buys and clever blending, Bill Nicholson had brought together a team capable of playing an exciting brand of football. Inspired by the inventive skills of their captain Danny Blanchflower and schemer John White, the non-stop aggression of Dave Mackay in midfield, the dash of Cliff Jones on the wing, and the bustling finish of Bobby Smith at centre-forward, the Spurs won their first 11 League games. They had the Championship sewn up with weeks to spare, and arrived at Wembley as hot favourites. They duly beat Leicester 2–0. They had captured the double — the 'Holy Grail' of English football.

Danny Blanchflower holds the Cup aloft at Wembley after the victory that gave the Spurs the 'double'.

Clay crashes to the canvas, felled by Cooper's devastating left hook at the end of the fourth round.

'enery's 'ammer

Cooper shuts Clay's big mouth but Clay is saved by the bell

When Cassius Clay came to Wembley in June 1963 to take on British heavyweight champion Henry Cooper, he had already earned a reputation as a 'big mouth'. Olympic light-heavyweight gold-medallist in 1960, he now had 18 straight professional victories under his belt in his drive towards the world heavyweight title. His 'poems', his abuse of opponents, and his uncanny predictions all went to making him the most colourful character in world boxing. True to form, he arrived in London in a blaze of publicity, referring to Cooper as a 'bum' and predicting a win in five rounds.

The Cockney Cooper, in complete contrast, was a gentleman, in or out of the ring. Modest and unassuming, he was one of the most popular of all British sporting figures and was universally admired and respected for his dignity and sportsmanship. Unfortunately, he had a tendency to cut easily, but he had tremendous courage and a devastating left hook known as ' 'enery's 'ammer'.

Clay's appearance in the ring in crimson dressing-gown and gold crown failed to impress the experienced Cooper, at 29, eight years older than the brash young American. Cooper's persistent jabbing seemed to worry Clay, but a cut over Cooper's left eye in the second round acted as a signal for Clay to begin his clowning. He got careless, and in round four Cooper saw his chance, moved in, and dumped Clay on the canvas with his famous left hook. For a few seconds Wembley went wild as Clay lay there open-mouthed and stunned. But then the bell went. Clay came out in the fifth and proceeded systematically to cut Cooper's face to ribbons. The referee had to stop the fight. Clay had fulfilled his prediction, and was on his way to a crack at the world title. But who knows how his career would have turned out had not the bell saved him from the effects of 'enery's 'ammer?

A Triumph for Sportsmanship

It is often said that the Olympics are too nationalistic, that all the flag-flying and anthem-playing tends to cloud the sporting traditions of the Games. And while it is true that partisanship adds a flavour to sporting contests, it often goes too far. This is increasingly so, as evidenced by all the violence in and outside soccer grounds, the drug-taking to improve performance, and even the cheating. For these reasons, it is particularly gratifying to look back on an incident that took place at the Winter Olympics of 1964.

The Italian bobsleigh driver Eugenio Monti arrived at the Innsbruck Games as the supreme champion — five straight two-man world titles from 1957 to 1961 and another in 1963, and four-man championships in 1960 and 1961. Yet he had been denied an Olympic gold medal, because there was no bobsleigh event at the Squaw Valley Games of 1960.

Great competitor though he was, first and foremost he was a sportsman. And it was an act of sportsmanship unheard of in modern times that contributed to his defeat in Austria. Among his most dangerous rivals in the two-man event were the British pair Tony Nash and Robin Dixon, whom he had greatly helped and encouraged before the Games. After the first of the four runs, the Britons were lying second. But their axle had broken and they had no ready replacement. So Monti, after finishing his second run, whipped off his own axle and gave it to Nash.

The British pair again came down in the second-fastest time, and the following day went on to win the gold, with Monti third behind Italy's second bob. Monti's crew won a bronze in the four-man event, too.

Bobsleigh gold-medallist Tony Nash (left) is congratulated by Italian rival Eugenio Monti, whose sporting act had made the British victory possible.

It was a famous British victory, their first ever in bobsleigh, but happily it was not the end of the Monti story. Four years later, at the Grenoble Games, Monti, now 40, won both the Olympic bobsleigh gold medals to crown his long and outstanding career. And never was a triumph so well-deserved, nor so popular with fellow competitors.

Willie Away!

Wilson Whineray climaxes a magnificent All Blacks tour

'Willie Away!' was the cry that went up when Wilson Whineray, All Blacks captain and prop-forward got the ball. These were the All Blacks of 1963–64, with forwards who ran and passed like backs — Whineray, the legendary Colin 'Pinetree' Meads, the strong-running Kel Tremain, and the fleet-footed Maori flanker Waka Nathan — and a goal-kicking phenomenon at full-back, Don Clarke. These Fifth All Blacks rampaged through Britain and France, losing only one and drawing one of over thirty matches.

It is now February 15, 1964, and Cardiff Arms Park is the scene of their farewell match against the Barbarians. Forgotten is the discipline that took them through their all-conquering tour. Forwards and backs are playing with an abandon associated more with their multi-national opponents. Unbelievably, as they pile up try after try, the Welsh crowd are urging them on: 'More! More! More!'. Suddenly, New Zealand centre Paul Little picks up a loose ball, darts forward, finds Whineray alongside, and passes. Some 60,000 Welshmen are on their feet at the sight of this mighty front-row forward taking the ball like a three-quarter, surging forward, and racing for the line with team-mates on either side. It is All Blacks rugby at its most spectacular, and leading the charge is one of the most popular captains to tour the British Isles.

Wilson, who has not scored on the tour, is expected to pass, but he sells the Barbarian full-back the perfect dummy and races through to score near the posts.

The noise from the crowd is deafening. Welshmen who have come to see the pride of British rugby bring down the All Blacks accord the New Zealand captain a reception few of their own heroes have received. As Whineray walks back and Clarke comes up to make the score 36–3, thousands of voices begin to sing: 'For he's a jolly good fellow'. And when the final whistle blows, bringing the tour to an end, Whineray is hoisted onto the shoulders of his team-mates and chaired from the field to a momentous ovation.

An emotional moment as Whineray is chaired from the field.

British Long-Jump Double

Mary Rand and Lynn Davies both strike gold in the Tokyo Olympics

No British athlete had won an Olympic long-jump title before Tokyo. In fact, you had to go back to 1908 to find the last British gold medal in the field events. So when British long-jumpers finished first in both the men's and the women's event in one Games, it was more than just a coincidence, it was a minor sensation.

Four years earlier, in Rome, Mary Rand (then Mary Bignall) had failed to qualify for the last six. This time, she made no mistake, breaking the Olympic record with her first attempt. And she proceeded to beat that Rome mark with her six jumps in the final. Only the Pole Irena Kirszenstein threatened her, and each time she was pressed Mary Rand pulled out a really big one to draw away again. She finally demoralized the opposition with a world record leap of 6.76m (22ft 2¼in) in the fifth round to win by 16cm.

Mrs Rand was the first ever British woman to win an athletics gold medal (Ann Packer joined her six days later when she won the 800m), and she won a silver in the pentathlon and a bronze in

Lynn Davies (above) and Mary Rand (left) leaping to Olympic glory.

the 4×100 metres relay.

Lynn Davies's victory a few days later was due to his ability to produce his best at the right time. Up against athletes whose best performances were as much as 30cm longer than his, he had the courage and determination to pull out all the stops at the crucial moment.

The favourites for the event were the American holder of the title and the world record, Ralph Boston, and European champion and previous world-record holder Igor Ter-Ovanesyan of the USSR. Both had marks of over 8.30m (27ft 2¾in) to their credit.

The morning of the long jump was very wet and windy, and after a sleepless night Davies made a mess of his first two

qualifying jumps. He realized in time that he had measured his run-up all wrong, and managed to qualify with his last effort. Now he felt fine.

It was still raining for the final in the afternoon. After four rounds Davies was lying third. As he stood at the end of the runway for his fifth jump, he saw the flag at the top of the stadium go limp — that meant the wind had dropped. He hurtled down the runway, hit the board, and soared into the lead with 8.07m (26ft 5¾in), a distance his two rivals could not quite match on the day.

So Davies, from the little village of Nantymoel, had done it. He was the first ever Olympic champion from Wales. No wonder they called him 'Lynn the Leap'.

Colin Cowdrey catches Neil Hawke to provide Trueman with his 300th Test wicket, and (inset) is the first to congratulate him.

Fred's 300th Test Wicket

'Line and length' comes the almost weary advice over the radio waves in a rugged Yorkshire accent. Test match commentator Freddie Trueman just cannot believe the waywardness of the England fast bowlers. Time and again he repeats the formula, 'Line and length', as he gives his terse inter-over comments. For it was by bowling a perfect line and length that Trueman amassed his 307 Test wickets.

That might sound boring or dull, but Trueman was no plodder. Far from it. They didn't call him 'Fiery Fred' for nothing! Trueman might have earned an early reputation as a ferocious speed merchant, but he soon realized that pace alone was not the be-all and end-all of fast bowling. He developed an ability to move the ball in the air and off the seam at speed, and could surprise the world's best batsmen, especially with his vicious

late outswinger or his famous 'yorker', and sometimes with a well-disguised slower ball. As a result, Trueman was able to stay at his peak until 1963, when, at 32, he took 34 wickets for England against West Indies.

By this time, he was easily the biggest wicket-taker in Test history, with 284. Against the Australians the following year he took his tally to 297, but was dropped for the fourth Test, and it was feared that his Test career might have come to an end.

Happily, however, he was recalled for the Oval Test. And although he was ineffective at first, he came on just before lunch on the third day and took the wickets of Redpath and McKenzie with successive balls. He failed to get his hat-trick after lunch, but it was not long before he had Hawke caught in the slips for his historic 300th Test wicket.

Hancock's Try

The 1965 Calcutta Cup match between England and Scotland at Twickenham was coming to an end with Scotland 3–0 up and attacking. Andy Hancock was standing on England's left wing, having received only two passes the whole match — and dropped them both!

The Scottish attack broke up and fly-half Micky Weston threw the ball out to Hancock deep in his own '25'. This time Hancock caught it, and set off along the touchline. He evaded two tackles and began his surge for the line. He just held off the last despairing Scottish tackle before flinging himself over. The match was only drawn, and anyway had no bearing on the Championship. But the 95 yards (87m) covered was the longest run-in for an international try.

Arkle the Wonder Horse

Arkle (right) and Mill House in the 1965 Cheltenham Gold Cup.

For a horse that was so superior to all his contemporaries, Arkle generated an unbelievable amount of excitement among his fans, of whom there were many. For never has there been such a popular chaser, such a horse so loved by the public, first in his native Ireland and then by racegoers everywhere. He captured the public imagination to such an extent, whether they were race fans or not, that when he was recovering from the injury that ended his career he received 'get well' cards from all over the world.

Arkle was trained in Ireland by Tom Dreaper, who bought him as an ungainly three-year-old for Anne, Duchess of Westminster, at the 1960 Dublin sales for a mere 1,150 guineas. At the end of 1961, Arkle, as a gelding, ran two undistinguished flat races. In 1962, he won four of his six hurdle races. He was partnered in two of these by Pat Taaffe, who rode him throughout his steeple-chasing career. This began at Cheltenham in November 1962, when Arkle won the Honeybourne Chase.

Returning to Cheltenham the following March, Arkle won the Broadway Novices Chase by 20 lengths, a couple of days before the English champion Mill House won the Cheltenham Gold Cup. Mill House was regarded as one of the great steeplechasing champions, but the rapidly improving novice Arkle was to ensure that he never won the Cheltenham Gold Cup again.

However, when Mill House beat Arkle in the Hennessy Gold Cup in November 1963, giving him 5lb and an 8-length beating into third place, the increasing talk of a 'wonder horse' was put down to Irish 'blarney'. But Arkle had stumbled three fences from home, and this cost him the race.

Both horses won their next three races, and then came the showdown, the 1964 Cheltenham Gold Cup, the championship of steeplechasing. Mill House started favourite at 13-8 on, with Arkle 7-4. In an epic race, the big Mill House led for most of the way, but when Arkle passed him coming up to the last fence the English champion had no more to give. Arkle sailed over and went on to win by five lengths.

Make no mistake about it, Mill House was a great horse, perhaps one of the top dozen steeplechasers of all time. But Arkle was in a class of his own. He confirmed this the following year, when he beat Mill House by 20 lengths in the Cheltenham Gold Cup, and in 1966 he chalked up a hat-trick. In handicap races, he was set to give massive amounts away to the rest of the field, and his rare defeats were all due to the handicapper. No horse on level terms ever got near him again. His final race was the King George VI Chase at Kempton Park on Boxing Day 1966. As usual giving away chunks of weight, he was sensationally beaten a length by Dormant. But it was discovered that Arkle had finished lame, with a broken bone in his foot! After months of speculation, it was decided not to run him again. There will never be another Arkle.

Grandpa wins the Derby

Leading Australian jockey Scobie Breasley arrived in England in 1950 at the age of 36 to start a new career. And by the time he was 50, and a grandfather, he had achieved as much success in the home of racing as he had in his native land. But like that other veteran, Gordon Richards, 11 years earlier, the greatest prize of all had eluded him, the Derby. So when he won it at last in 1964 on Irish horse Santa Claus (left), it was an immensely popular victory. And he went on to win it again two years later.

Clarke's historic 3 miles in 1965.

King without a crown

Australian runner Ron Clarke was a 'king without a crown'. He set 17 world records in the mid-sixties, from 2 miles to 20,000m, but he never won a major international title. In Olympic and Commonwealth Games throughout the sixties, he won silver and bronze or finished further down the field to runners with inferior times to his.

Yet some of his records were phenomenal, clipping huge chunks off long-established marks. One of his most memorable runs was at London's White City in July 1965, when he became the first man to break 13 minutes for the 3 mile race.

What a come-back!

In what has been described as the most thrilling golf match of all time, Gary Player came back from being 7 down with 17 to play against the American Tony Lema. It was the 36-hole semi-final of the Piccadilly World Match Play Championship at Wentworth in October 1965. Still 5 down with 9 to play, Player finally drew level with a superb birdie at the last hole, and won at the first extra hole. He beat Peter Thomson 3 and 2 in the final.

'It's a Fix!'

'It's a fix!' was the cry that went up after both of Sonny Liston's controversial defeats by the loquacious Cassius Clay. For what other heavyweight champion had lost his title sitting in his corner? And who saw the mysterious punch that laid Liston flat on his back after less than a minute of their second fight? The two contests must rank among the most sensational even in a division of the sport where sensations abound.

'Ahm gonna whup that ugly bear' was Clay's pre-fight taunt, but few who had seen that 'ugly bear', ex-convict Liston, in action regarded it as anything more than an act of bravado, a piece of the now customary Clay clowning to whip up public interest. And there were many who felt that the bombastic Clay would finally get his 'comeuppance', that Liston who had twice demolished Floyd Patterson inside a round, would shut his 'big mouth' for good.

At the weigh-in for the first fight, on February 25, 1964, Clay apparently went berserk, ranting and raving like a madman. The medical officer in charge expressed his doubts as to Clay's sanity and felt he was scared to death. This did not appear so when Clay got into the ring — until round five, that is, when Clay kept rubbing his eyes, complaining that he could not see. He had to be forced out of his corner for round six. Quite remarkably he then proceeded to give the puzzled champion a boxing lesson, and it was Liston who sat on his stool at the end of the round and refused to come out. It eventually needed a panel or eight doctors to issue a statement that Liston had suffered a shoulder injury before the cries of 'Fix!' subsided.

In the return, 15 months later, Clay, or Muhammad Ali as he now was, knocked Liston out with a short right to the jaw — so short that few people saw it — after just 60 seconds. The cries of 'Fix!' started up again almost before Liston hit the canvas . . . and they have never subsided.

Ali stands snarling over the prostrate Liston as their second fight approaches its controversial finish.

World Cup Drama

Was the ball over the line?

Above: **Bobby Moore with the triumphant England team. Hurst is on his right.** *Left:* **The controversial goal — the ball has bounced down off the bar. Was it over the line?**

There is little doubt that England deserved to win the 1966 World Cup. But their vital third goal in the final, scored in extra time, remains controversial to this day, and the West Germans have always insisted that it should never have been allowed. What they forget is that the free-kick that enabled them to equalize in the 90th minute and take the match into extra time was perhaps even more dubious.

England started marginal favourites, but an early uncharacteristic error by Ray Wilson allowed the Germans to take an unexpected lead through Haller. A few minutes later, however, England were on level terms, Geoff Hurst

80

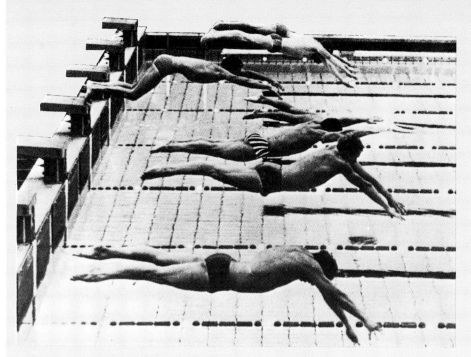

McGregor is left at the start in the European 100m final.

Driving Double

The Ferraris were clear favourites for the French Grand Prix at Reims in 1966. But the winner was Australian driver Jack Brabham, who had won the race six years earlier, also at Reims, in a Cooper-Climax. What made the 1966 race so special, however, was the car Brabham was driving — a Brabham! Thus he became the first driver to win a grand prix in his own make. It was a remarkable accomplishment, for he not only had to drive in races all round the world, but was busy inbetween times building, preparing, and maintaining the cars. Brabham went on to win both the drivers' and the manufacturers' world championships — a unique achievement.

Gold at last for McGregor

Scottish swimmer Bobby McGregor went to Utrecht for the European Championships in August 1966 knowing that this was probably his last chance of a major title. He had dominated British sprint swimming for five years and broken the 110yd world record four times, but a gold medal had always eluded him.

Twice runner-up in the Commonwealth Games and narrowly beaten in the Olympics, McGregor found his greatest 'opponent' at Utrecht was the starter. McGregor lined up on the blocks in lane 5. First, the Russian to his right lost his balance and wavered. Then the East German on his left also wobbled, and anticipating the gun got a 'flyer'. McGregor, expecting a recall, was still on his block when the other seven were in the water. But without panicking he steadily caught up to be level at 50m, and drew away to win by a metre — for his first gold medal.

heading in a long free-kick from West Ham club-mate Bobby Moore.

England got on top after the interval, with Moore's anticipation and calming influence at the back and Alan Ball's incessant running. They took a well-earned lead in the 78th minute through Martin Peters. The Germans appeared to be on their knees and it looked all over, when out of the blue Weber scrambled an equalizer following a hotly disputed free-kick. Manager Alf Ramsey calmed his players before the start of extra time, and just told them to 'go out and do it again'.

The controversial incident occurred in the 10th minute of extra time. The indefatigable Ball, after a long chase to the right, pulled the ball back to the ever-available Hurst, who hooked it hard against the underside of the bar. Did it drop down over the line? Roger Hunt thought so, spinning round and leaping for joy. The Germans thought differently. The referee was not sure, but his Russian linesman was, and a goal was given.

The Germans were beaten and demoralized, but Hurst made sure of England's victory with a spectacular solo goal in the dying seconds to complete his hat-trick, unique in a World Cup final.

Eusebio v North Korea

The surprise of the 1966 World Cup was North Korea, who sensationally beat Italy to qualify for the quarter-finals. There, they met the star of the tournament, Portugal's Eusebio. And the match turned out to be just such a confrontation: Eusebio versus North Korea. In just 25 minutes, the unknowns from the East with the strange-sounding names were three up. But that was when Eusebio, the 'Black Panther', decided to take matters into his own hands. He began to run the ball at the Koreans. He scored two before the interval and two more in the second half. The final score was 5–3.

Campbell Dies on Lake Coniston

Bluebird breaks up at 300mph

Campbell in *Bluebird* the car (1962).

The fatal crash — *Bluebird* 'takes off' on Coniston.

Donald Campbell took over breaking records where his father Sir Malcolm left off. The American Stanley Sayers had beaten his father's water speed record, so with his father's boat, *Bluebird*, and the same crew, Campbell won it back in 1955 on Lake Coniston, the same water. At 202.32mph (325.59kph), he was the first man to exceed 200mph on water. Five more times in the fifties he beat his own record. Then in 1964, he again emulated his father by beating the land speed record, one that had stood for 17 years. With 403.01mph (648.58kph), he was the first man to exceed 400 miles an hour on land.

In 1967 he returned to Coniston for a further crack at the water speed record in a jet boat, another *Bluebird*. After clocking 297mph (478kph) on the downward run, he was coming back even faster, when suddenly the boat literally took off and crashed down into the lake. He was perhaps within a second of the magic 300mph. Donald Campbell's body was never found.

Unsung Champions

Bernard Ford and Diane Towler won the British, the European, and the World Championships of their sport four years in succession, from 1966 to 1969. Wherever they appeared abroad, they were acclaimed by press and public and fêted on TV. Yet at home they were largely ignored and their achievements rarely honoured. For they were ice dancers. They had reached the top in a field that was barely acknowledged as a sport in Britain. They themselves attributed this lack of home recognition to a certain confusion in the sporting media about the word 'dance'.

After their fourth triple triumph in 1969, they were both awarded the MBE. They then turned professional, and that year won the world professional championships. Ice dancing became an Olympic sport in 1976.

A Victory for Football

Celtic open the 'padlock'

Celtic (green) have finally breached the Italian defensive wall, with a cracking goal from full-back Tommy Gemmell (No. 3, partially hidden).

After the heady days of Real Madrid and Benfica, the European Cup in the mid-sixties looked set for a period of domination by the defence-minded Italian clubs. AC Milan won it in 1963 and Inter-Milan in 1964 and 1965. Real Madrid had returned to snatch the trophy once more in 1966, but now Inter were in the final again, up against Celtic who were making their first appearance in the competition.

No British side had reached the final before, but Celtic, guided and inspired by their former captain Jock Stein, had just completed a marvellous domestic season, winning all three major Scottish trophies.

Under Stein, whose motto was 'The best place to defend is in the other side's penalty box', Celtic played an all-out brand of 'total football' years before the Dutch were credited with inventing it. They had eleven 90-minute players. Their support for the man with the ball and their running off the ball were prime facets of their play, but teamwork was never allowed to obscure individual brilliance. They possessed two fine overlapping full-backs in Jim Craig and Tommy Gemmell, and the mastery of their captain Billy McNeill in the air was evident at both ends of the field. In midfield they had the power and all-round skills of Bobby Murdoch and the guile of Bertie Auld. And up front they

had the genius of that fiery little winger Jimmy Johnstone.

Inter were Italy's finest exponents of 'catenaccio', the 'padlock' defence, which employed a sweeper behind the back four. They played a cat-and-mouse type of game, and when they snatched the lead there was no better team at sitting on it.

So when Inter went ahead in the final at Lisbon from a 7th-minute penalty, Celtic were faced with an uphill fight. They immediately set about their task with determination and no little confidence. They won control of the midfield, and began to push men forward from the back. Even so, the half-

time whistle went and they still had not penetrated the famous Inter rearguard.

Far from discouraged, though, they came out in the second half and threw wave after wave of attack at the Italians. At last the wall was breached, when Tommy Gemmell came up to hit a searing drive into the net from over 20 metres. There were still 28 minutes left — 28 minutes of torture for the Italians, who were completely overrun. With five minutes to go, Steve Chalmers deflected a Murdoch shot into the net for Celtic's winner. Attacking soccer had triumphed. It was a wonderful win for the Scots, and even more, it was a victory for football.

Close for Killy

Alpine ski racer Jean-Claude Killy won all three gold medals at the Grenoble Winter Olympics of 1968, equalling Toni Sailer's achievement of 1956. But Killy, a Frenchman who grew up on the Alpine slopes, did not enjoy Sailer's superiority, having less than a tenth of a second to spare in both the slalom and the downhill. An exciting and fearless racer, he shunned caution even to protect a big lead. And the closeness of his victories in those Grenoble Games was a tribute to his nerve and sheer competitiveness.

Dream Debut

At Cardiff Arms Park in April 1967, an 18-year-old fresh out of school lined up against England to make his Welsh debut. A centre for Newport, Keith Jarrett was playing out of position at full-back. By the end of the game, he was a national hero, having kicked two penalties and converted five tries, including a brilliant one he scored himself. His record 19 points swung the game for Wales, who won 34–21.

Colin Meads, rugby's greatest forward, is sent off against Scotland.

Meads sent off

The first player to be sent off in a rugby union international was All Black tourist Cyril Brownlie, against England at Twickenham in 1925. The 'Brownlie Incident', as it became known, caused a furore, and it is said that the Prince of Wales, who was attending the match, tried unsuccessfully to have the New Zealand forward returned to the field. Despite playing for 72 minutes with only 14 men, the All Blacks won 17–11 to complete their unbeaten tour.

It was 42 years before another player got his marching orders in a test. And again it was an All Black forward, Colin 'Pinetree' Meads, this time against Scotland at Murrayfield. New Zealand's most capped player and a giant of rugby in every way, Meads was warned first and later sent off for a second serious infringement. The incident caused another stir. It could be argued that Meads, penalized for aiming a kick at the Scottish fly-half as he was about to pick up the ball, was legitimately going for the ball. Anyway, the All Blacks again won (14–3), and went on to complete their second unbeaten tour.

The perfect pair

Pairs skating has been an Olympic event since 1908, but few people could name any pairs skaters before the mid-sixties. That is when the Russian husband and wife pair Oleg Protopopov and Ludmila Belousova (who used her maiden name for skating) revolutionized the sport with their balletic style of skating.

Renowned for their graceful high lifts and the one-handed 'death spiral' in which Ludmila's hair just brushed the ice, the Protopopovs won their first Olympic title in 1964 and for the next four years won both the world and the European titles. They reigned supreme in their sport, and their crowning glory came in the 1968 Olympics. At the ripe old age for skaters of 35 (Oleg) and 32 — for neither had started until 16 — they earned 5.9s (out of 6) from eight of the nine judges for artistic presentation and from six for technical merit.

The Protopopovs, the Russian pairs skaters who won universal acclaim and popularity in the 1960s for their classic style of skating.

Champions at Last

Ten years after Munich, Bobby Charlton leads United to European triumph

In a match highly charged with emotion, Manchester United became the first English side to win the European Cup when they beat Benfica 4–1 at Wembley in May 1968. It was a win acclaimed by football fans all over Europe, whatever their allegiance. For this was the side that had risen out of the ashes of the Munich air disaster ten years earlier to challenge once again for the highest honours.

In their manager, Matt Busby, they had the 'father figure' of British football, a man loved and respected throughout the game. In the mid-fifties, he had built an outstanding side, the 'Busby Babes', who were carrying all before them before they were destroyed in the tragic crash. The disaster had occurred when the team were returning from Belgrade, having just reached the semi-finals of the European Cup. Busby himself was almost killed in the crash. Another survivor was Bobby Charlton, now United's captain. Probably England's best-loved footballer, he had been one of her World Cup heroes in 1966.

United's finest match of the 1968 European campaign was in the semi-finals in Madrid. Bringing only a slender 1–0 lead from Old Trafford, thanks to a George Best goal, they were soon up against it and by half-time were 3–1 down. But a stirring second-half performance was climaxed by two Best-made goals in the last 18 minutes, the winner coming from centre-half Bill Foulkes, another Munich survivor.

The final, appropriately, was at Wembley. With all of Britain and most of Europe willing them on, and with so much at stake, it is not surprising that United made a hesitant start. It was one of their lesser lights, left-winger John Aston, who impressed most in a colourless and scoreless first half. But after a calming half-time talk from Busby, United came out and Charlton scored with a header almost immediately. They could not add to their lead, though, and Graca stunned them with an equalizer nine minutes from time. It was only Stepney's reflex save from Eusebio in the dying moments that kept them alive.

Then, in extra time, Best took all the pressure off his weary colleagues with a brilliant solo goal. Kidd and Charlton added two more. Tears of joy flowed at Wembley and all over Europe that night.

Right: **An emotional Bobby Charlton in Madrid after United clinch a place in the final for the first time.** *Below:* **Best puts United ahead in the final after a run from the half-way line.**

Six of the Best

It was a summer evening in 1968 at Swansea, where Glamorgan were playing Nottinghamshire in an end-of-season County Championship match. The Notts captain Gary Sobers sauntered to the wicket with 308–5 on the board. The great West Indian all-rounder hit 76 not out in 35 minutes. But his innings is remembered for one over, in which he smashed every ball from spinner Malcolm Nash for six. The fifth ball was caught, but to the delight of the crowd the fielder had stepped over the boundary. Nash tried a seamer for his sixth delivery, but Sobers hit it clean out of the ground.

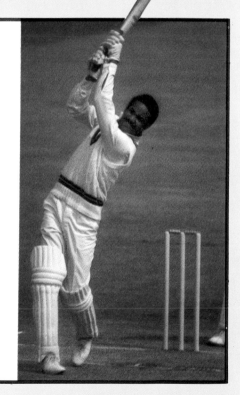

One of These Days....

Beamon leaps into the next century

'One of these days', they used to say about American long-jumper Bob Beamon, 'if everything goes right, he'll jump out of the pit'. Well, Beamon didn't quite clear the long-jump pit in the 1968 Olympics, but his phenomenal leap will probably keep him in the record books until the next century.

In the final of the long jump, the first three contestants fouled. Beamon came bounding down the runway, hit the board, and then soared into the thin air of Mexico City to break the sand too far for the sighting device to be used. Out came the steel tape, as someone ventured that it must be all of 28 feet, the next 'magic number' in the long jump list of world records. Suddenly Beamon is seen cavorting with joy as the figures light up on the scoreboard — 8.90 metres. The commentators cannot believe their conversion tables — 29ft 2½in. That was 1ft 9½in (55cm) farther than anyone had jumped before. The competition was over with the first jump.

Czech triumph

There was a great deal of sympathy and support for Czech athletes at the Mexico City Olympics, after their country had been occupied by the Soviet armies, especially where rivalry with Russian competitors was concerned. So gymnast Vera Caslavska was the darling of the crowd as she won four individual gold medals. And she brought the house down when she performed her floor exercises to the 'Mexican Hat Dance'.

Flopping to victory

A 21-year-old American student Dick Fosbury captured the imagination of the sporting world when he introduced his new style of high jumping at the Mexico City Olympics. As the other 12 finalists, all using the orthodox straddle style, gradually dropped out, Fosbury emerged as the winner. With his curiously curved run-up and backward clearance of the bar, he jumped an Olympic record 2.24m (7ft 4¼in). His technique caught on, and now most of the world's leading jumpers use the 'Fosbury flop'.

Four-Timer

There is more to sporting success than speed or strength, skill or technique. The great competitor is the one who can produce his best at the right time, the one with the ability to pull out something extra when the 'chips are down'.

Al Oerter was the supreme competitor. An American discus-thrower, he won his first Olympic title as a 20-year-old in 1956. He upset the favourites by producing a personal best with his very first throw. He was often beaten between Olympics, but in 1960, this time as favourite, he produced another personal best to overhaul his team-mate Babka with his fifth throw. In 1964, in all sorts of physical trouble with a slipped disc and torn rib cartilages, he again shattered his opponents with a fifth-throw winner. And in 1968 he produced a lifetime best to record a unique achievement in Olympic history — a fourth gold medal in consecutive Games.

Oerter, who himself set four world records, beat the current world-record holder in each of his four Olympics. Other discus-throwers used to shudder at the mention of his name, and it was a relief to them all when he decided not to compete in 1972.

Right: **Oerter in the discus circle.**

Keino routs Ryun

Jim Ryun, world mile and 1,500m record holder, was unlucky that the 1968 Olympics were held 2,240m above sea level. But although his great rival Kip Keino had the advantage of coming from a high-altitude country, the Kenyan had already run the 10,000m and 5,000m (winning a silver). In the 1,500m final, Keino ran a courageous race, opening up a gap while the American stayed at the back. Ryun began to go through the field, but the Kenyan, running by himself for the last half of the race, kept relentlessly on. Ryun came after him, but Keino beat him into second place by some 20 metres.

The Perfect Result

Tie in Ryder Cup

It's a close one for Tony Jacklin.

British golfers had not won the biannual Ryder Cup since 1957. But as usual they came out at Royal Birkdale in September 1969 full of hope and confidence as they prepared to take on a strong American team.

Spearheaded by Tony Jacklin, fresh from his Open triumph, Britain emerged level after two days of foursomes. After the eight singles on the morning of the third day, they had a two-point lead, highlighted by Jacklin's 4 and 3 defeat of Jack Nicklaus. In the afternoon, however, the Americans soon squared the match, and with the last two matches on the course it was still level pegging.

Britain's Brian Huggett holed a nerve-tingling putt on the 18th to halve his match with Billy Casper, and for a moment thought Britain had won because of the roar from the crowd at the 17th. But that was for Jacklin holding a 17m putt to square with Nicklaus. On the 18th green, now, Jacklin was less than a metre from the hole, Nicklaus just over a metre. The big American coolly holed his putt despite large numbers of the partisan crowd 'willing' the ball out. For a moment, it looked as if Jacklin would have to hole what was in this situation a missable putt to save the whole contest for Britain. But in an instant, Nicklaus had scooped out his ball and conceded Jacklin's putt. This fine act of sportsmanship provided the perfect result — the first tie in Ryder Cup history.

Gonzales the Magnificent

American tennis star Richard 'Pancho' Gonzales was arguably the greatest player never to win Wimbledon, for it was as a professional that he was indisputably the world's No. 1 in the fifties. When tennis went 'open' he was 40, but in 1969 he ensured himself a place in Wimbledon folklore after the longest match in the history of the championships.

On the Centre Court, against the 25-year-old Charlie Pasarell in the first round, he saved 11 set points before succumbing 24–22 in the first set. Then, playing reluctantly in poor light, he petulantly lost the second set 6–1, and was actually booed off by a section of the crowd. Continuing the next day, he levelled the match with 16–14, 6–3 sets. But the 16-year difference was beginning to tell, and Pasarell came back in the final set. Behind Gonzales now, the crowd gasped in disbelief as he saved SEVEN MATCH POINTS and went on to win 11–9 — after a record 112 games.

Gonzales, at 41, refuses to give in.

Little Miss Runner-up

No longer runner-up, the victorious Ann Jones (left) with Mrs King.

Known as 'Little Miss Runner-up' after her defeats in all three 1957 world table tennis finals, Ann Jones (or Haydon, as she then was) turned to tennis. And despite winning the French title twice in the sixties, she continued to miss out so often that the name stuck. It seemed that her left-handed baseline game was not good enough for the fast grass courts at Wimbledon. Four times she raised British hopes when she reached the semi-finals, and four times she could get no further. In 1967, she reached the final, but was seen off by the champion, Billie Jean King.

It looked like the same old story when she faced No. 1 seed Margaret Court in the 1969 semi-finals and lost the first set 12–10. But she clawed her way back to win, and came back from a set down in the final, too, to beat the champion, Mrs King. She had well and truly lost that 'runner-up' tag.

Brave Lillian

Lillian Board captivated the sporting world with her personality and her courage on the track. In the late sixties, she was built up by the media as the new 'Golden Girl' of British athletics. As a result, she was under a lot of pressure in the 1968 Olympics, and it was a great disappointment when she was beaten on the tape by Colette Besson of France in the 400m.

In the 1969 European Championships, however, she really 'came good', winning a fine 800m and avenging her Olympic defeat by beating Besson on the tape in the 4×400m relay. Who knows what heights she would have attained had she not then been tragically struck down with cancer. She faced it with the same courage she showed on the track, and the world mourned when she died in December 1970 at the age of 22.

Pelé's 1,000th Goal

When today's top strikers struggle to score 30 goals in a season, it is a sobering thought that Pelé once hit 30 for his club Santos in 10 games over a five-week spell in 1961. In his glittering first-class career (1956–74) he amassed 1,217 goals in 1,254 games. His 1,000th goal was a landmark in the history of soccer, and the whole of Brazil watched and waited as he approached the magic number. When he scored it, from a penalty, in November 1969, the game stopped as the crowd streamed onto the Maracana pitch, and Pelé did a lap of honour before escaping to the dressing-room.

Pelé (right) slots in a penalty for Santos to record his 1,000th goal. The crowd went wild. Balloons were released carrying a placard proclaiming the feat, and the whole of Brazil celebrated. Pelé was mobbed, and had to be substituted before the game could continue.

Other great moments and exploits of the sixties

Roger Maris of the New York Yankees hit 61 home runs in 1961 to beat Babe Ruth's 34-year-old record by one.

Stuart MacKenzie, Australian oarsman, recorded his sixth successive victory in Henley's Diamond Sculls in 1962.

Graham Hill, driving a BRM, became the first Briton to win the world title in a British car, in 1962.

Donald Jackson of Canada gave perhaps the finest freestyle skating performance ever seen when he won the 1962 world title. Of the nine judges, six awarded him the maximum 6 for artistic impression.

Ove Fundin of Sweden won his record fifth World Speedway Championship in 1967.

Chuang Tse-tung spearheaded China's domination of world table tennis in the 1960s, winning the 3 singles titles from 1961 to 1965, as well as helping China win 3 Swaythling Cups before they disappeared for the rest of the decade.

Karen Muir, South African swimmer, became the world's youngest ever individual world record holder in any sport when she swam a 68.7sec 110yd backstroke at Blackpool in 1965 — at the age of 12 years 10 months and 25 days.

Jim Ryun set four middle-distance world records in the 1960s, including the mile in 3min 51.1sec and 1,500m in 3min 33.1sec, both in 1967.

Jack Nicklaus recorded seven 'big four' victories in the 1960s, including three US Masters in four years.

Tony Jacklin became, in 1969, the first 'home' winner of the British Open for 18 years.

John Surtees completed a hat-trick of both 350cc and 500cc world motorcycle titles in 1960, and then, turning to the four-wheel sport, won the World Drivers Championship in 1964 — a unique achievement.

Vyacheslav Ivanov of the USSR won his third successive Olympic single sculls gold medal in 1964.

Mike Hailwood, British motor-cyclist, won the world 500cc title for the fourth straight time in 1965.

Anton Geesink, a massive Dutchman, shattered the myth of Japanese invincibility in judo by winning the Open category in the 1964 Olympics in Tokyo.

Barry John

Jack Nicklaus

Pelé

Olga Korbut

Bjorn Borg

Rudi Hartono

Rodnina and Zaitsev

Giacomo Agostini

THE SEVENTIES

Terrorism and politics reared their ugly heads to cast a sinister shadow over the Olympic Games in the 1970s. In Munich in 1972, Palestinian terrorists caused the deaths of 11 members of the Israeli team, and four years later in Montreal the Black boycott led to the withdrawal of teams from some twenty nations. Fortunately, this misuse of a great sporting occasion as a world stage for political propaganda did not spread to soccer's World Cup, although the increasing violence in and around football grounds became a sickening sight in many countries.

On the bright side, Pelé confirmed his place as the world's greatest footballer with unforgettable performances in the 1970 World Cup. And he later came out of retirement to win the hearts of the American people, while Dutch star Johan Cruyff was the man who provided the thrills in the world's major competitions.

Another dazzling footballer was Welsh fly-half Barry John, the undisputed 'king' of rugby union. Other giants in their sport included Jack Nicklaus, who amassed more prize money and 'big four' titles than any other golfer, Italian motorcyclist Giacomo Agostini, who ran up a record number of world titles, and Soviet skater Irena Rodnina, who, with two partners, won a record number of pairs world titles. Indonesia's Rudi Hartono was to badminton and Wembley what Bjorn Borg was to tennis and Wimbledon. And two young girls enthralled the world with their gymnastic grace — Olga Korbut and Nadia Comaneci.

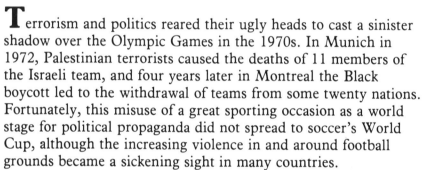

WORLD EVENTS OF THE SEVENTIES...Watergate scandal...end of Vietnam War...

restoration of Spanish monarchy... death of Mao Tse-tung... first Concorde flight...

Disbelief is etched on a thousand faces and Pelé stares in amazement as Banks deflects the ball to safety.

Save of the Century

When football fans look back on the 1970 World Cup in Mexico, they remember the inventiveness of Pelé, the explosive free-kicks, Rivelino's lethal left foot, the goals of Jairzinho and Müller. Yet among this wealth of attacking football, there stands out the memory of Gordon Banks projecting himself sideways and with a flick of his wrist stifling the shouts of 'Goal!' in 70,000 throats.

Gordon Banks, goalkeeper in England's World Cup winning side of 1966, had maintained his position as the world's No. 1, and now he was confirming it in the cauldron of Guadalajara against one of the finest attacks of all time. Brazil had already given the world a taste of their collective footballing genius with a scintillating 4–1 victory over Czechoslovakia. Now they were weaving their patterns round an England defence marshalled by Bobby Moore and anchored by Banks, a

master of the angles. It was a confrontation for the connoisseur.

The pass that started the move came from Brazil's captain and right-back Carlos Alberto and was described by Banks as 'like nothing I had ever seen before'. It curved diagonally across the field, round England's left-back Terry Cooper, and into the path of Jairzinho, running at full tilt. The right-winger made for the bye-line and, as Banks came to cover the near post, got in a remarkable cross under pressure to the far post. And there was the unmarked Pelé, soaring into the air, and powering a header down and into go- . . . but no, Banks was there, having danced across his goal, and now desperately flinging himself across as the ball bounced in front of the goal-line, and flicking it up on the half-volley with the palm of his hand, up and over the bar.

Pelé said it was the greatest save he had seen. No one would argue with that.

Pelé's Dummy

As memorable as any of the goals in the 1970 World Cup finals are Pelé's near misses, in his quest for the 'impossible': his shot from behind the half-way line, his lightning volley from a goalkeeper's clearance, and above all his famous dummy in the semi-final against Uruguay.

Tearing onto a diagonal ball from the left, with the keeper rushing out, he let the ball run. The keeper, Mazurkiewicz, was left stranded, with the ball whizzing past him on his left and Pelé on his right. Pelé 'put on the brakes', cut back behind the keeper, and then just screwed the ball past the far post as the Uruguayan defenders were coming back to cover.

The Court-King Epic

Margaret Court during her epic final.

When Margaret Court met Billie Jean King in the Wimbledon ladies' singles final in 1970, it was a true clash of the giants. The two, who dominated the ladies' game in the 1960s, had met in the final before, in 1963. And the then Miss Margaret Smith had beaten the then Miss Billie Jean Moffitt 6–3, 6–4. For the remainder of the 1960s, one or other of them had reached the final.

Tall, powerful, and wonderfully athletic, Mrs Court was the outstanding Australian woman player of all time. Yet throughout her career, in which she won more major titles than any other woman, she occasionally suffered lapses of confidence. She never forgot the time when, as top seed at Wimbledon in 1962, she had been put out by the young and virtually unknown Miss Moffitt. Mrs King, on the other hand, was always bursting with confidence, and despite her lack of inches played a strong serve-and-volley game.

When the two ladies came onto Wimbledon's Centre Court in 1970, they were both nursing leg injuries. Yet they produced the longest set played in a Wimbledon singles final.

Three times Mrs King served for that first set, but Mrs Court never allowed her to get within a point of winning it. At 11–12, Mrs King had a set point against her — and saved it courageously with a drop shot. But after 1hr 27min Mrs Court finally won the set 14–12.

She was wearing her opponent down with her power play, so in the second set the American began using the drop shot more. It was an enthralling match, as Mrs King tried to break up Mrs Court's game. But there was no stopping the Australian, although Mrs King saved a match point at 6–7 and then, quite remarkably, another four at 9–10, before going down 9–11. The match lasted 2hr 26min and a record 46 games. Who knows when it would have finished had

a third set been necessary.

Later that year, Margaret Court, who had already won the Australian and French titles, added the US title to complete the 'grand slam' of women's tennis, something only the great Maureen Connolly had done.

'Fight of the Century'

Frazier is sent to a neutral corner after flooring Ali in the 15th.

Billed, not uniquely, as 'The fight of the Century', the Frazier-Ali clash in 1971 was the first ever title bout between two undefeated heavyweight champions. Ali had been stripped of his title in 1967 because of his refusal to join the US Army. Joe Frazier had won the WBC version of the world title in 1968, but it was not until 1970, when he stopped Jimmy Ellis in five, that he was universally recognized as the champion.

Constantly moving forward, Frazier was an all-action fighter, prepared to take any amount of punishment provided he could get in his damaging lefts to face and body. In the early rounds, Ali showed no signs of being ring-rusty, but he began to get caught on the ropes more as the fight went on. And apart from the ninth, when Ali suddenly came out and gave Frazier a boxing lesson, the champion was clearly on top. He even dropped Ali for a count of three in the last round, and he won a unanimous decision.

'A hell of a man is Barry John'

Above: **McBride wins the ball for the Lions in the crucial third Test.** *Below:* **Barry John's kicking helped him amass a record 180 points from his 16 games on the tour, where he was the inspiration of the Lions, the first British Isles side ever to win a series in New Zealand, the stronghold of rugby union.**

Magnificent Lions win 'down under'

'A hell of a man is Barry John' wrote the bard at the Eisteddford, and he echoed the sentiments of rugby men everywhere. John had returned from New Zealand the hero of heroes, the star of the magnificent British Lions who had for the first time beaten the All Blacks in a series. It was not so much the victory, but the manner in which it was gained, that earned the tributes. They won in style, with adventurous attack, disciplined defence, and perfect teamwork. And above all, their free-running game reflected the sheer joy of playing rugby.

The man behind the Lions' triumph was coach Carwyn James, and the backbone of the side was Welsh, too, with captain and centre John Dawes, Gareth Edwards partnering John at half-back, and the exciting J. P. R. Williams at full-back. Other stars from other countries included centre Mike Gibson and second-row forward Willie John McBride of Ireland, prop Ian 'Mighty Mouse' McLauchlan of Scotland, and winger David Duckham of England.

Comprehensive British victories in the early matches of the tour did little to shake New Zealand confidence in the might of the All Blacks. But when the Lions won the first Test 9–3 at Dunedin, it sent a shock wave through the whole country. And although the All Blacks were rampant again with a solid 22–12 win at Christchurch, it was not for long. That man Barry John got to work at Wellington with a dropped goal in three minutes. He then converted a try by Gerald Davies from the touchline and scored and converted his own try. The Lions ran out 13–3 winners and so were 2–1 up with one Test to play.

The climax came at Eden Park, in a cut-and-thrust match full of drama. The Lions, 0–8 down, drew level. Then they led 14–11, but the All Blacks equalized six minutes from time. Those were six long minutes for the Lions, but they held out — and returned home to a rapturous reception. And Barry John was 'the King', not only for the 30 points he scored in Tests, but for the way he would control a match with his line kicking, his probing punts, his elusive bursts, and above all that uncanny instinct of the true champion for doing the right thing at the right time.

The chubby features of Marie-Therese Nadig (above) belied her athletic skill on skis. She won the Olympic downhill (right) as well as the giant slalom.

Swiss schoolgirl's shock ski triumph

The first Winter Olympics to be held in Asia took place at Sapporo, Japan, in February 1972. There were several surprises, not least the slalom victory of Francisco Fernandez-Ochoa, the first Spaniard to win a medal of any kind in a Winter Games.

But pride of place must go to a chubby Swiss schoolgirl of 17, Marie-Therese Nadig. Without a previous race victory that season, Miss Nadig skied superbly. She just pipped hot favourite Annemarie Proell of Austria to win both the downhill and the giant slalom. A fall in the special slalom robbed Miss Nadig of further honours, and Miss Proell's fifth place in this event was enough to earn her the overall world championship. But the Austrian had to wait another eight years for her Olympic revenge and a gold medal in the downhill.

World Champions of Tennis

Rosewall-Laver clash scales heights of tennis perfection

The World Championship of Tennis, launched in 1971, was a million-dollar circuit of 20 tournaments linked by a points system. The eight leading players took part in a final tournament for a then record prize of $50,000. In the first final, Ken Rosewall beat Rod Laver in four gripping sets.

Now the same two Australians, who had dominated professional tennis in the sixties, are to contest the second final, at Dallas in May 1972. The players come out in tropical indoor heat, heightened by banks of TV arc-lights. The frail-looking Rosewall seems as if he is going to wilt, especially when Laver takes the first set. But Rosewall, using all his guile and speed across the court, seizes the initiative. With marvellous ground-strokes and courageous returns, he destroys Laver's first serve and breaks up his game. After taking a 2–1 lead, however, he finds himself slowly drooping in the heat, and Laver takes the fourth set on a tiebreak.

Rosewall's last chance appears to have gone when, in a breathtaking final set, Laver battles his way to 5–4 on another tiebreak, with his serve to come. Rosewall reaches back nearly 20 years, for the inspirational backhands that endeared him to Wimbledon fans as a 17-year-old. He finds one, then another. Now he has match point. Laver nets his return; game, set, and match to Rosewall 4–6, 6–0, 6–3, 6–7, 7–6. And 20 million viewers have just witnessed tennis perfection.

Wimbledon Magic

Smith–Nastase classic

Although many of the world's leading players were barred because of their contracts with World Championship Tennis — including Laver, Rosewall, and the holder for the previous two years John Newcombe — Wimbledon produced a great men's final in 1972.

Pitted against each other were Stan Smith and Ilie Nastase. Smith, a corporal in the US Army, was the top seed. A towering, gangling man, he possessed a rare mobility for a player of his size. Nastase, a touch player, was the No.2 seed and the most entertaining player on the circuit. He lacked power, but a far greater shortcoming was his temperament.

And on Wimbledon's Centre Court against Smith, it was his temperament that let Nastase down. He reached the height of his bewitching artistry in the first and fourth sets, and inbetween plumbed the depths of uncertainty as he debated line calls, conversed with spectators, and swore at his racket, which he frequently changed. The crowd were behind the volatile Romanian, but the impassive US corporal earned their respect with his courage and sportsmanship. Nastase finally conquered himself in the fifth set, but he could not subdue his opponent. In a nerve-tingling finale that had the crowd frequently on its feet, Nastase saved three match points before he went down. The score in Smith's favour, was 4–6, 6–3, 6–3, 4–6, 7–5. As the crowd roared their appreciation, Smith, generous in his moment of triumph, put his arm round the dejected Nastase. Surely, his time would come.

Sadly, it didn't. The Romanian's court behaviour degenerated into appalling displays of pique and childishness. He never allowed his game to fulfil its mercurial promise. And he started a trend of disgraceful court manners, carried on by the boorish behaviour of his doubles partner Jimmy Connors and, later, the unforgivable excesses of John McEnroe.

Massie's Match

Bob Massie in action against England at Lord's.

Never has there been a better instance of the right man for the right moment than Bob Massie's Test début in 1972. The conditions at Lord's for the second Test were ideal for the prodigious swing of the 25-year-old Australian medium-pace bowler. In both innings it was Dennis Lillee, making his first tour, who unsettled England's front-line batsmen with his speed before Massie, with his skilful control of length, ran through the brittle English batting.

Massie followed his 8 for 84 in the first innings with 8 for 53 in the second. His match figures of 16 for 137 were by far the best ever for a Test débutant, the best Australian figures in a Test, and the third best analysis in Test history.

Massie took only another seven wickets in the series, which was drawn. It was Lillee who matured into a great bowler, whereas Massie, after two more Tests against Pakistan that year, disappeared from international cricket.

Mary Peters, flanked by Heide Rosendahl (left) and third-placed Burglinde Pollak, captivated the crowd with her joyous personality.

The Munich Olympics began as 'The smiling Games', but there were few smiles left after the Arab terrorists struck. Two girls whose charm and performance lit up the Olympic scene, however, were Olga and Mary.

Olga

The Russian champion Ludmila Turistcheva won the women's overall gymastics title at Munich, and an East German won two of the individual golds. But the girl who stole the limelight — Olga Korbut — was a Russian reserve who took part only because one of the team was taken ill. The impish Olga, 17 and standing 1.52m (5ft), won the hearts of the crowd in the gymnastics hall and enchanted millions of television viewers around the world with her coquettish performances — and she also won two golds.

Mary

A bubbling blonde from Belfast, Mary Peters was almost twice Olga's age. She was competing in her third Olympic pentathlon, and this was her last chance of a medal. On the first day, Mary was second in the hurdles and first in both shot and high jump. The high jump was the crucial event, because she needed to build up a big lead to take into the second day, when her great rival, West German Heide Rosendahl, would have her best events. And even the partisan German crowd warmed to Mary's charm and courage as she twice cleared the bar at her third attempt and then went on to produce a personal best. The next day, Rosendahl almost equalled her own world record in the long jump, but Mary still led going into the last event, the 200m. And she clung on for dear life to produce another personal best and remain ahead — by just 10 points, in a world-record total of 4,801. The whole crowd began chanting her name. There can rarely have been such a popular winner on foreign soil.

Olga won gold on floor and beam.

96

World-record holder Jim Ryun trips in his heat of the 1,500m and is eliminated. Thanks to the failure of the US authorities to point out that the time submitted for Ryun was for the mile (not the 1,500m), he was unseeded, and found himself in the most frantic heat.

American Disasters

A striking feature of the 1972 Olympic Games in Munich was the comparative eclipse of the Americans. By normal standards, 33 gold medals cannot be termed a failure, but compared with the 50 of the Russians and the 33 shared by the Germans (20 East, 13 West), the American achievement was their worst for a very long time. Yet it could not so much be attributed to falling standards as to slack organization and the most dreadful bad luck. It seemed as if there was an imp — a whole army of imps — sitting on their shoulders just waiting for an opportunity to wreak some mischief.

Two American sprinters, joint world record holders for the 100m, arrived too late for their heats and were eliminated. Jim Ryun got himself boxed in during his heat of the 1,500m, tripped, and was out. Dave Wottle completely misjudged his semi-final run and failed to qualify. And although he won the 800m, he found, to his acute embarrassment, that he had worn his white golf cap during the US national anthem. But the antics on the rostrum of two Black American medal-winners in the 400m, who deliberately ignored their anthem, echoing the Black Power protest of 1968, earned them immediate banishment from the Games, and the US were unable to field a 400m relay team.

Further disaster hit the Americans in the pole vault. The champion and world-record holder, Bob Seagren, found at the last moment — but after a long-drawn-out controversy — that his pole was banned. He was unable to get used to the standard pole in time, and could only finish second. Thus the United States lost the pole vault for the first time in Olympic history.

And although the Americans won 17 of the 29 swimming golds, they were still not without their troubles. Their 400m winner, Rick DeMont, an asthmatic, was disqualified for taking a prohibited drug, something the American team doctors should have spotted.

But the most dramatic setback of all for the United States is their defeat, for the first time ever in the Olympics, in the basketball. Not such a dominating force in Munich, they are struggling manfully in the final against the Russians, who have led for most of the match. They creep up to within a point with only seconds to go. The Russians, shaken, miss a basket, and Doug Collins races to the other end with the ball before he is sent sprawling. Stunned, he finally gets up after an agonizing interlude and makes the two free throws. With only 3 seconds left on the clock, the score is USA 50 USSR 49. The Russians restart the game and the final buzzer goes — but the clock still shows 1 second. The referee orders another restart, the buzzer sounds again, and the court becomes a mass of celebrating American players and fans, their proud record apparently intact after a fairytale finish.

Then, an announcement to clear the court becomes ominously persistent. It appears that the 3 seconds have to be replayed. As the players take up their positions again, the Americans can barely comprehend the situation. From under his own basket, Ivan Edeshko throws a court-length pass to the tall Alexander Belov. He catches it as two Americans guarding him collapse in a heap, and pops it in as the buzzer goes for the last time — USSR 51 USA 50. The 'imp' has struck again, and the fairytale ending has turned into an American nightmare.

From Failure to Fantasy

Mexico City flop becomes Munich hero

It might seem a fantasy of the highest order to win seven gold medals at one Olympics. But that's just what American swimmer Mark Spitz did at Munich in 1972. And it must rate as an even more fantastic achievement when you consider his comparative failure four years earlier. Then, as an 18-year-old at Mexico City, he had been favoured to win six gold medals, but came home with 'only' two, in the relays, and an individual silver and bronze.

But he put all the disappointments and uncertainty behind him as he stood on the starting block for his first final in Munich, the 200m butterfly. The tall, lean American, sporting a wicked 'Zapata' moustache, slipped into top gear as soon as the race began. Inexorably he built up a lead, until he came home with two seconds to spare in a new world record. So the haunting

disasters of the last Games were exorcized with one crushing swim on the first day of the programme. Less than an hour later he was the anchor man in the US 4×100m relay team, which won in world-record time.

And so it went on. In eight days of competition, with only one rest day inbetween, he swam 13 races, including heats. The 200m freestyle was followed

by the 100m butterfly and the 4×200m relay. More victories, more world records — there was no stopping Spitz and his American team-mates. After the rest day, he won the 100m freestyle, the 'blue riband' of swimming, and finally swam the butterfly in the medley relay for his seventh gold medal and his seventh world record. It was a feat without parallel in Olympic history.

'The Try'

Cultured Barbarians score try of tries against All Blacks

Ask any rugby man about 'the try' and it's odds on he will tell you about the one the Barbarians scored against the seventh All Blacks at Cardiff in 1973. After a successful, if controversial, tour,

in which the New Zealanders' dour, 'safe' football had not won them many friends, this last match was like a fifth international. The Barbarians, at least in the back division, were virtually a

British Lions side. Barry John had retired, but at fly-half was his 'heir apparent', Phil Bennett.

And it was Bennett who began 'the try', after only two minutes. Running back deep into his own '25' to gather a cross-kick, he turned and sidestepped one man, then two more, before passing to full-back John Williams. He squirmed out of a tackle to get it to hooker John Pullin, who in turn found skipper John Dawes. Dummying at speed up the left to the half-way line, Dawes gave it inside to forward Tom David, who, riding a tackle, passed to the No. 8 Derek Quinnell. All this interweaving and interpassing had been accomplished at great speed. Suddenly, seemingly out of nowhere, up came Gareth Edwards to take the ball and fly past what was left of the All Blacks' cover to score in the corner with a spectacular dive. The rest of the match was an exhibition as the All Blacks joined in the spirit of things, and the Baa-Baas ran out 23–11 winners.

Dawes (13) commits Syd Going (9) before passing to David. Quinnell (headbanded) and try-scorer Edwards are on the right.

Miller Magic

The scene is Oakmont, Pennsylvania, the date June 17, 1973, and some ten golfers are battling for the lead in the last round of the US Open. Suddenly a score goes up on the boards around the course. Johnny Miller has posted a record 63. It is like a race where the chief contenders are so busy watching each other that they do not notice the outsider coming from behind until it is too late. Weiskopf, Palmer, Trevino, and Nicklaus — none of them can catch Miller. At last the 26-year-old Californian has won a major title.

Tall and blond, with boyish looks, Miller had failed to live up to his early promise, earning a reputation for 'blowing hot and cold' — spoiling his good rounds with a bad one. He had blown up in the US Masters two years before, and this is what looked like happening at Oakmont, when he carded a third round 76 that put him apparently out of contention in 13th place — that is, until his storming finish.

Strangely, Miller's career also blew hot and cold. He opened the 1974 season with three straight wins, won eight tournaments in all and broke the record for prize money. He ran away with the first two tournaments in 1975, shooting a 61 in each of them. He popped up again in 1976 to snatch the British Open with a final round of 66. He has done little since, but you can never discount Johnny Miller.

Hole in One

The man who stole the show on the first day of the 1973 British Open was 71-year-old US veteran Gene Sarazen, winner of the Open back in 1932. He holed his tee shot at the 8th!

The evergreen Mr Murphy

Alex Murphy never ceased to confound the critics with both the longevity of his career and his quest for honours. He toured Australia as far back as 1958, and was in Britain's World Cup winning side in 1960. With his quicksilver bursts and defence-splitting passes, half-back Murphy figured in St Helens' Cup and Championship victories of the 1960s.

The unquenchable Murphy — 'Alex the Great' — holds the Rugby League Challenge Cup aloft in 1974 after leading his third club to victory.

Then, apparently in the twilight of his career, he went to Leigh as player-coach and led them to their 24–7 Challenge Cup win over Leeds in the 1971 final.

Still he wasn't finished. Two seasons later, he moved to Warrington as manager-player-coach. And in 1974, he was back at Wembley, inspiring them to a 24–9 triumph over Featherstone. It was his fourth final, his fourth triumph. And 13 years after his first appearance there, he maintained his record of having scored in all of them.

World Cup Winner

British soccer fans remember German striker Gerd Müller for the goal that knocked England out of the 1970 World Cup. The stocky, mobile Bayern Munich star was top-scorer in that tournament with 10 goals, but West Germany could finish only third.

Now it was four years later, and West Germany, the host country, had reached the final in Munich. Müller had scored three, including the winner against Poland in the semi-final.

The final had a dramatic opening, with the Germans a goal down in 78 seconds — before they had touched the ball. They were up against a brilliant Dutch side, spearheaded by the exciting Johan Cruyff. And it was Cruyff who picked the ball up in his own half and

Müller (right) swivels to hook the ball home for the World Cup winner.

raced into the German penalty area only to be pulled down. Neeskens scored from the spot. But after 25 minutes the Germans were awarded a penalty, from which Paul Breitner equalized.

The winner came two minutes before half-time, and Müller scored it typically from a half-chance. Lurking near goal,

he took a low cross and hooked it into the far corner of the net. It was a simple goal, scored with deceptive ease by a man with a gift for goals. And it was his 14th World Cup goal — an all-time record.

Artist on Grass

Ashe blunts Connors' power

After Jimmy Connors' comprehensive Wimbledon victory in 1974, when he demolished veteran Ken Rosewall 6–1, 6–1, 6–4 in the final, he seemed destined to remain the world's No.1 for many years. Brash, ill-mannered and childish on court, the 20-year-old American nevertheless possessed boundless

courage and determination to go with his power game. He hit the tennis scene like a whirlwind, brushing opponents aside with his relentless hitting. Left-handed and with a double-fisted backhand, he attacked the ball ruthlessly and retrieved it brilliantly.

Hot favourite to retain his title in

1975, he more than justified his No.1 seeding by reaching the final without losing a set. There, he faced the No.6 seed, fellow-American Arthur Ashe, whom he had beaten in their last three meetings. Ashe, a fine sportsman and a popular figure, was now nearly 32, and few gave him a chance of surviving for long against Connors' overwhelming power.

But Ashe never allowed Connors to settle into the rhythm that made him so lethal. Using all his guile and court-craft, he stretched Connors with wide-angled shots, had him twisting and turning with delicate lobs to the backhand corner, and destroyed Connors' service with the accuracy and variety of his returns. Above all, he denied Connors the pace he so relishes for counter-hitting. Ashe raced away with the first two sets 6–1, 6–1. Connors bravely came back to take the third 7–5 and then led 3–0 in the fourth. Had Ashe finally shot his bolt? No, he continued to play with his head, broke back to level at 3–3, and took the set 6–4. It was, perhaps, the greatest upset in Wimbledon history.

Ashe turns to the crowd after his sensational defeat of the champion.

What a Race!

The Grundy-Bustino duel at Ascot in 1975 has been described by many racing people as the greatest horse-race they have ever seen. Eleven runners lined up for the valuable 1½-mile King George VI and Queen Elizabeth Diamond Stakes, but there were only two in it at the finish. Grundy, fresh from his victories in the Derby and Irish Derby, was the slight odds-on favourite, with Bustino, the 1974 St Leger winner, next in the betting, followed by Dahlia, a two-time winner.

With two pacemakers setting a furious gallop, Bustino took over the running four furlongs (½ mile) out. Joe Mercer drove him on in an attempt to blunt Grundy's renowned finishing burst. Pat Eddery, two lengths adrift on Grundy,

Grundy (10) finally conquers Bustino as they near the winning-post.

set about closing the gap. There was no blistering acceleration — the pace was too fast — but a sheer, slogging grind up the straight. With a furlong to go, it was neck and neck, and then Grundy edged ahead to win by half a length, smashing the course record by a massive 2½ seconds.

Artist on Ice

Curry brings a new dimension to skating

John Curry's style of skating was frowned upon in certain circles, especially among East European countries. He was first and foremost an artist on ice, but his critics felt his programme was not masculine or athletic enough. After finishing second to a Russian in the 1975 European Championships, Curry himself attacked the communist-bloc judges for biased marking.

Under the guidance of coach Carlo Fassi in America, Curry began to have more confidence in himself. He introduced more athleticism into his programme, building it around his jumps. He first won the European title, and then at Innsbruck, in the 1976 Winter Olympics, he gave a glittering display of skating. Perfectly executed jumps and beautiful spins allied to his moving interpretation of the music left no doubts in the minds of the judges. He was in a class of his own, and finished streets ahead of a clutch of other contestants to win Britain's first medal in the Winter Games for 12 years. He went on to win the world title before turning professional.

Artistry on ice — John Curry at the 1976 Winter Olympics.

101

Viren Outfoxes them All

The magic moment as Lasse Viren outsprints a clutch of fast finishers to retain his second title and win his fourth Olympic gold. New Zealander Dick Quax (691) is second, while his compatriot Rod Dixon (689) is edged out of a bronze by the West German Hildenbrand, who throws himself over the line. Britons Brendan Foster (364) and Ian Stewart (380) are 5th and 7th, respectively.

When Lasse Viren won both the 10,000m and 5,000m Olympic titles in 1972, he turned the clock back fifty years, to the days of the great Nurmi and the rest of the 'Flying Finns'. His 10,000m victory was quite remarkable because he fell half-way through the race, but recovered to win in world-record time.

Viren did little of note in international competition in the intervening years, suffering numerous defeats. But as soon as he set foot on an Olympic track again, at Montreal in 1976, he seemed to be transformed. In the 10,000m, he took the lead with just over a lap to go and loped home to retain the title. Only the great Zatopek had done that before. The 5,000m was packed with good runners, all determined to beat the champion, but in the end he outfoxed and out-sprinted them all to retain his second title. And not even Zatopek had done that.

Little Miss Perfect

A 14-year-old Romanian gymnast Nadia Comaneci replaced Olga Korbut as the 'darling' of the 1976 Games. But she did not arouse quite the same emotions as her Russian rival, because she was just too perfect.

Performing her routines like a little mechanical doll, she shattered the confidence of the Russians in the compulsory exercises with a superb display on the asymmetrical bars. It earned her 10 points from the judges — the first perfect score in the history of Olympic gymnastics. On the second day of the team event she obtained two more maximums, for the bars again and for the beam. But Romania could not break the Russian stranglehold on the team event, and she had to be content with silver.

No one could stay with her in the individual events, though. She received two more perfect scores on the bars and another two on the beam, and won the two gold medals. Only Nelli Kim, who achieved two maximums and won the

vault and floor titles, provided a challenge. But she could not prevent the precocious Romanian winning the overall title — her third gold medal.

Below: The scoreboard is not equipped to show the first perfect score in Olympic history. Nadia went on to win gold for the bars, the beam (right), and the combined.

102

Cheat!

The biggest sensation of the Montreal Games occurred early one morning in the fencing hall, on the second day of the modern pentathlon. In the most exhausting of the five disciplines, all the competitors (47 in Montreal) fence each other in a gruelling 12-hour competition. Each bout is 'sudden death', the first hit winning. Fencers fight their team-mates first, and then the competition is organized in a series of 'matches', with one country against another.

In the first encounter, between Britain and the USSR, Adrian Parker protested when a hit was recorded against him in his bout with Boris Onischenko. The judge checked the circuits and confirmed the hit. But both Parker and team-mate Jim Fox were certain that the Russian's épée had not touched him. So when Fox faced Onischenko, he feinted to lunge and then drew back as the Russian's blade moved forward. The light came on, but there was no question of a hit. Onischenko agreed, and tried to change his weapon. Fox, in the belief that it was short-circuiting (he did not dream it had been tampered with), insisted it be examined.

Weapon control dismantled Onischenko's épée and discovered a sophisticated push-button circuit-breaker that allowed him to record a hit at will — in other words, to cheat. Onischenko, silver-medallist and leading fencer in Munich, was disqualified and sent home in disgrace.

The whole episode left a very bad taste — and several questions unanswered. Not least of these was: could Onischenko have done this without the knowledge of the Russian authorities?

The Winners

The British victory in the team event was a sensation in itself, for they had never won a medal of any sort in modern pentathlon. Admittedly, with Onischenko's disqualification, the holders and favourites were out. But an easy course took away the British advantage in riding, and Fox, shattered by his unwitting part in the disgrace of a long-time respected rival, fenced badly. It required a superhuman effort by all three in the last event, the cross-country. They provided it — and won the gold medal.

Top right: **Fox insists that the suspect weapon be examined.** *Top:* **The light recording a hit is on (far left) as Onischenko (left) lunges at Fox.** *Centre:* **Fox is still fighting, knowing he has not been hit.** *Below:* **Officials and onlookers cluster round as the offending weapon is examined.** *Right:* **A happy ending for the victorious British team, Parker (left), Nightingale, and Fox.**

The Centenary Test

Randall pulls Lillee to the boundary during his memorable knock.
Inset: The scoreboard at the close of England's heroic 2nd innings.

The 'clown prince' of cricket, Derek Randall earned a reputation for being a marvellous entertainer, especially in the field. And despite an unorthodox shuffle in front of his stumps, his batting earned him an England place. He chose the Centenary Test against Australia, at Melbourne in March 1977, to play his most exciting innings.

After dismissing Australia for a paltry 138 in the first innings, England were themselves skittled out for 95, Lillee taking 6 for 26. The Australians then amassed 419 in their second innings, thanks largely to a swashbuckling unbeaten hundred from keeper Rod Marsh. It left England 463 runs to get, a task that had never been achieved in a Test. Inspired by Randall, England went for the runs. He hit his maiden Test century and finished up with a magnificent 174. England, all out for 417, were beaten by 45 runs. But it was a glorious defeat.

Ginny at Last

'Jubilee' champion

It was Virginia Wade's 16th Wimbledon. They said she was past it. The 31-year-old British girl, who had won the US title in 1968 and been up and down the world rankings like a yo-yo, had always disappointed at Wimbledon. Twice she had reached the semi-finals, another four times the last eight. The pressure on Britain's 'only hope' was always intense, but now, in 1977, after a wonderful win over the champion Chris Evert, she was in the final.

It was not a classic. Her opponent, the Dutch veteran Betty Stove, as surprised as anyone to find herself there, was as nervous as Ginny. But she took the first set 6–4, and it began to look like the 'old, old story', especially when Miss Wade lost a 3–0 lead in the second. But she pulled herself together and won the last two sets 6–3, 6–1. At last she had conquered Wimbledon. And what a time to do it — in the Centenary Championships and the Queen's Jubilee year.

A jubilant Ginny after receiving the trophy from the Queen.

Farewell Pelé

Pelé's farewell match, in which he played one half for New York Cosmos and one for his old club Santos, was sprinkled liberally with typical American 'show-biz schmaltz'. But through all the razzamatazz shone Pelé's sincerity. Three years earlier, he had come out of retirement, and with his unrivalled skills, wonderful sportsmanship, and above all his great love of the game had brought it to a nation that had more than once rejected the sport. In his three seasons with Cosmos, Pelé 'sold' soccer to the States. It wasn't so much his tricks and his goals that captured the public imagination, but his bubbling enthusiasm and his natural humility. At the end of his farewell game, he ran a lap of honour with a Brazilian flag in one hand and an American one in the other. Already a national hero in his own country, he had become a hero of a whole continent. It was a great moment for sport.

A Hundred Hundreds

England and Yorkshire opener Geoff Boycott had ensured his place in cricket history long before that summer evening at Headingly when he completed his hundredth century in front of his own adoring fans. Over 15 years he had gradually, with unshakable dedication, developed from a solid technician into a batsman of the highest Test calibre. He had also acquired an unfortunate predisposition for controversy, perhaps because of his singlemindedness. To his admirers, he was the greatest batsman in the world; he could do no wrong. But his critics felt he put himself before the side, and that his batting, although prolific in his accumulation of runs and records, was limited. There was also the little matter of his self-imposed exile from Test cricket for three years — at a time when the Australian fast bowlers Lillee and Thomson were at their fastest and most dangerous.

Boycott had returned to the fold only the previous Test, at Nottingham, where he had scored 107 and 80 not out and batted on all five days. Now, at Headingly, when he completed his historic century, the crowd went wild and stopped the match for nearly ten minutes. Boycott, who was the first player to reach this milestone in a Test, went on to make 191.

Boycott on-drives Greg Chappell to the boundary for his historic 100.

Despite terrible facial injuries, Lauda returned to regain his crown.

Lauda's comeback

World champion in 1975, Austrian racing driver Niki Lauda met with a horrifying crash at the notorious Nurburgring in the German Grand Prix the following year. Trapped in his blazing Ferrari, he suffered dreadful facial burns. Incredibly, six weeks after receiving the last rites in hospital, he was back on the track. But in the end he had to concede his title to James Hunt — by one point!

Now, in 1977, he was the champion again, winning by a comprehensive 17 points. It was a comeback almost unparalleled in sport — a triumph for willpower and courage.

Great Britain

Britain had chalked up fine Wightman Cup wins in 1974 and 1975, but against depleted American teams. The 1978 triumph, however, was earned against the full tennis might of the Americans. And it was as dramatic as it was unexpected. Inspired by Michele Tyler's win over Pam Shriver, Virginia Wade and Sue Barker both beat Tracy Austin and then combined in an electrifying decider to beat Shriver and Chris Evert in the final set.

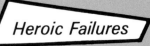

India's Final Flourish

King of the Jungle

Severiano Ballesteros won the 1979 British Open in remarkable style. As he zigzagged his way from tee to green, he rarely made contact with the fairways. He seemed always to be playing out of sand or rough. No wonder they called him 'King of the Jungle'.

A first round 73 had left the young Spaniard eight strokes off the lead, but a blistering 65 on the second day put him second. None of the other leaders could match his unorthodox consistency, and his last-round 70 was enough to give him a three-stroke margin over Jack Nicklaus and Ben Crenshaw. At 22, he was the youngest champion this century.

At the end of a dismal tour in which their only victory was against bottom county Glamorgan, India came miraculously close to tying the Test series with the highest fourth innings score ever made to win a Test. England, one up with two Tests drawn, set India 438 to win in 500 minutes at the Oval in the fourth and last Test. And thanks to opener Sunil Gavaskar they very nearly pulled it off.

First with Chauhan and then with Vengsarkar, Gavaskar flayed the English bowlers until he was fourth out at 389. With three balls left any result was possible. But it was just too much for the gallant Indian tail-enders, and at 429 for 8 they were eight runs short of victory.

Gavaskar made the highest score for an Indian against England, 221.

Other great moments and exploits of the seventies

Ivan Mauger of New Zealand completed a hat-trick of World Speedway Championships in 1970, a unique feat.

Princess Anne won the European equestrian championships in 1971 on Doublet.

Arsenal achieved the League and Cup double in the 1970–71 season.

Graham Hill, in 1972, added the Le Mans 24-hour race to his Indianapolis 500 victory of 1966 and his two world titles to complete a unique treble in motor sport.

Rudi Hartono of Indonesia won the All-England Badminton Championship for the 7th straight time in 1974 and for a record 8th time in 1976.

Jackie Stewart took his tally of major grand prix successes to a record 27 in 1973, and retired after winning his third World Drivers Championship.

British Lions, led by Willie John McBride, beat South Africa 3-0 in the Test series, and claimed they were robbed of a 100% tour record when the referee disallowed a last-minute try and the final Test was drawn.

Kornelia Ender, 17-year-old East German, won 4 gold medals at the 1976 Games, a record for a woman swimmer.

Eddy Merckx, Belgian cyclist, won his fifth Tour de France in 1974, equalling Frenchman Jacques Anquetil's record.

Reg Harris, world professional cycling sprint champion of the early 1950s, came out of retirement in 1974, and at 54 won the British professional 1,000m title, beating men half his age.

Alberto Juantorena of Cuba achieved the first ever 400m/800m double at the 1976 Olympics in Montreal.

Muhammad Ali became the first heavyweight to regain the world crown twice. He beat George Foreman in 1974, and then lost the title and won it back from Leon Spinks in 1978.

Gary Player, at 42, became the oldest man to win the US Masters when he carded a record-equalling last-round 64 in 1978 and made up 8 strokes on the leader to win by one.

Mike Gibson, in 1979, beat fellow-Irishman Willie John McBride's records by winning his 69th cap for Ireland (best for any country) and playing in his 81st international (including 12 for the Lions).

Red Rum became the first horse to win the Grand National three times. His record in 5 runs (1973–77) was 1, 1, 2, 2, 1.

Hank Aaron of the Atlanta Braves retired in 1976 with a major league career record of 755 home runs.

Ovett and Coe

Steve Davis

Sugar Ray Leonard

John McEnroe

Ed Moses

Severiano Ballesteros

Ian Botham

Diego Maradona

THE EIGHTIES

Overshadowing the sporting scene at the beginning of the 1980s was the controversy over the Moscow Olympics, which eventually led to another substantial boycott. Whatever the rights and wrongs of the political debate, one thing is perfectly clear. The very administrators who complain about politics interfering with sport are themselves the culprits for allowing the Games to be used for propaganda purposes — as Hitler did in 1936. Will they never learn?

With America, West Germany, Japan, Kenya, and several other nations missing, many events were devalued. A 400 metre hurdles, for example, without Ed Moses is unthinkable, as the 1976 champion continued to dominate an event as no other athlete has ever done before. Two valid contests were the Ovett–Coe clashes, and the two record-breakers continued to set new world marks and beat all-comers after the Games.

In tennis, the brilliant John McEnroe at last broke Bjorn Borg's stranglehold on the Wimbledon title, but set new lows in court behaviour. Another new face emerged in snooker, but with a familiar name, Steve Davis. Ian Botham set the cricketing world alight, while his Somerset colleague West Indian Viv Richards continued to delight the fans as the world's No. 1 batsman. Severiano Ballesteros continued to play swashbuckling golf, welterweight Sugar Ray Leonard lit up the boxing scene, and Argentinian Diego Maradona emerged as the most exciting footballer since Pelé.

WORLD EVENTS OF THE EIGHTIES ...Russians in Afghanistan... assassination attempts

n President Reagan and the Pope... assassination of Egypt's president Sadat... Space Shuttle launched...

Golden Jubilee

England stopped over in India in February 1980 to play the Golden Jubilee Test in Bombay. And although they won by 10 wickets, it required a sterling stand by Ian Botham and Bob Taylor and some record-shattering performances by the same pair to turn the game England's way. The two came together with England a feeble 58 for 5 in reply to India's first innings 242. With a sixth-wicket record of 171, they took England on the way to a comfortable lead. Botham made a brilliant 114.

It was in India's second innings that the records really began to tumble. Botham took 7 for 48 to add to his first innings analysis of 6 for 58, and became the first player to take more than nine wickets and score a century in a Test match. Meanwhile Taylor was in fine form behind the stumps. Having equalled the Test record with seven catches in the first innings, he took another three to set a new record of 10 dismissals in a Test. Eight of his catches were off the bowling of his partner in crime, Botham.

Another wicket for the record-breaking pair as Gavaskar falls for the second time to the bowling of Ian Botham (far right) and catching of keeper Bob Taylor (far left).

Yet despite these world records and Botham's gargantuan performance, the incident that will perhaps be remembered longest was a gesture from Indian captain Viswanath. With England struggling at 85 for 5, Taylor, on 7, played and missed and was given out, caught at the wicket, the only 'appeal' having been a casual look at the umpire by the bowler. Viswanath, after consulting his fellow-slips, persuaded the umpire to rescind his decision — an act of the highest sportsmanship seen all too rarely in international sport.

American triumphs at Lake Placid

The 1980 Winter Olympics were held at Lake Placid, in upstate New York, and the host country enjoyed two triumphs on the ice that stood out above all the other feats of the Games.

One was an individual achievement, unique in the history of winter sport — five gold medals. Eric Heiden, 21, had been world speed skating champion for three years, and soon became a familiar sight at Lake Placid in his skin-tight golden racing suit. In nine days he won the 500m, 5,000m, 1,000m, 1,500m, and finally a world-record 10,000m.

In complete contrast, the US ice hockey team were given scant hope of beating the mighty Russians. But in an emotionally charged atmosphere they produced the biggest upset for years to triumph 4-3. It then needed another superhuman effort to beat Finland 4-2 and clinch the gold medal.

The Taming of a Bully Boy

Moving up from the lightweight division, Roberto Duran from Panama challenged American 'golden boy' Sugar Ray Leonard for his welterweight crown at Montreal's Olympic Stadium in June 1980. Duran, at 29, had an impressive record, with 70 wins (55 of them by knock-outs) in 71 fights. But the 24-year-old Leonard was the favourite. Olympic gold medallist in 1976, he had won all of his 27 professional contests, 18 of them inside the distance.

In the ring, Duran was a cross between Marciano and Frazier. He hurled himself at Leonard in spells of unbridled aggression. The American responded with brilliant combinations of punches. But Duran kept coming forward relentlessly. Apart from the occasional mid-round breather, they seemed to spend round after round standing toe-to-toe and slugging it out at a furious pace. Leonard got on top as Duran tired around the 12th and had him in trouble. But still the Panamanian shuffled forward and threw himself at the champion in two-fisted brawling assaults. And after 15 frenetic rounds, he earned a unanimous decision. Leonard had lost his first fight, but took the lion's share of the purse — $7½ million out of a record $9 million.

The return five months later in New Orleans was watched by some two million viewers on closed-circuit TV across America and around the world. It turned out to be even more sensational than the first fight — but for very different reasons. This time, Leonard managed to keep the fight at a distance. He adapted his tactics to his opponent's techniques and completely demoralized Duran with his ringcraft and his menacing left hook. He taunted him with his own version of the 'Ali shuffle', pulling faces and sticking out his chin.

Suddenly, however, near the end of round eight, Duran stopped fighting. He did not appear to be hurt, but he just gestured that he had had enough — like a theatregoer leaving a poor performance in the middle of the second act. He explained later that he was suffering from body cramps and could not move properly. But the only feasible explanation appeared to be that this tough 'bully boy' of the ring just could not stomach the public humiliation Leonard was subjecting him to. Leonard was certainly ahead at the time, but Duran was virtually unmarked. Here was a champion nonchalantly conceding his crown and walking off with ten million dollars. It was the most unaccountable capitulation since Sonny Liston's seventeen years earlier, and it cast a similar sinister shadow over the 'noble art'.

Leonard (right) taunts the demoralized Duran in their second fight.

Nicklaus Back on Top

At 40, Jack Nicklaus was surely coming to the end of his reign at the top of world golf. Competing less now, the 'Golden Bear' was facing increasingly stiff opposition from young lions such as Tom Watson at home and Ballesteros from abroad.

Any suggestion of impending retirement, however, was dispelled on the Baltusrol course, New Jersey, in June 1980, scene of the US Open. In the first round, Nicklaus went out and shot a record-equalling 63, to share the lead with Tom Weiskopf. Over the next two rounds, Nicklaus struggled to keep ahead, while Weiskopf fell away completely. Now, on the last day, Japan's Isao Aoki was level, with others in strong contention. But within three holes, Nicklaus had grabbed a lead of two, and he was equal to all challenges. He finished with two birdies to clinch his 16th major title. It was a record-equalling fourth US Open and his 272 beat the championship record by three strokes. Nicklaus was well and truly back at the top.

Wimbledon's Greatest Final

Borg's fifth triumph

Bjorn Borg earned himself sporting immortality when he won his fifth straight Wimbledon title in 1980. After nearly four hours of breathtaking, cliff-hanging tennis, he finally subdued the young American John McEnroe. The 21-year-old McEnroe had saved seven match points in an extraordinary fourth set that included a 20-minute tiebreak. But, as he said ruefully afterwards about the winner: 'When he loses a tiebreak like that and he's won the tournament four times, you'd think maybe he'd let up . . .' Well, perhaps ordinary mortals would finally have capitulated — but not the imperturbable Swede.

McEnroe serves for the fourth set during the historic tiebreak.

Borg sinks to his knees in victory.

The start of the match had been disastrous for the champion, with McEnroe racing away to win the first set 6–1. Borg seemed unable to handle the American's powerful, swinging service. The first crisis came at 4–4 in the second set, when Borg had to save three break points in a long game on his own service. He finally broke McEnroe's service to take the set 7–5.

After saving several break points on his service, Borg took the third set 6–3. And when he stood at 5–4 in the fourth

set and 40–15 on his own service, it looked all over. But now it was McEnroe's turn to show his steel, and indeed his genius as he saved the match points with two brilliant and daring passing shots. Soon the set had moved forward to the unforgettable tiebreak, as each of the two gladiators in turn gained the ascendancy and the other refused to lie down. McEnroe saved five more match points, while Borg saved six set points before he succumbed to the seventh and lost the tiebreak 18–16.

Unbelievably, Borg came out even stronger for the final set. He dominated his own service, and with a searing double-handed backhand took McEnroe's in the 14th game to win 1–6, 7–5, 6–3, 6–7 (16–18), 8–6. At last, he could sink to his knees in that now familiar gesture of triumph and relief.

Cawley's Comeback

The ladies' Wimbledon final in 1980 was contested by two former champions, both married to Britons and both stylish and highly popular players. Mrs Cawley had first won the title as an unsophisticated 19-year-old in 1971, Evonne Goolagong. And now she won it again, beating Chris Evert-Lloyd 6–1, 7–6 in a delightful match — after three final defeats, a series of injuries, and the birth of a daughter in the intervening years.

The Ovett and Coe Show

Britain's record-breakers share the spoils

Six days after his defeat by Ovett in the 800m, Coe gains his revenge in the 1,500m, with Ovett third behind the East German Straub.

Yifter the Shifter

Continuing the great tradition of Ethiopian distance running begun by Abebe Bikila 20 years earlier, Miruts Yifter pulverized the opposition in both the 10,000m and 5,000m to bring off a magnificent Olympic double. Standing only 1.60m (5ft 3in), this balding little man of indeterminate age (35 to 39 is the accepted range) becomes a giant of the track. There are three Ethiopians in the 10,000m and they burn off most of the opposition with regular surges. Only the Finns stay with them, and although Maaninka is second, the great Viren comes fifth, beaten at last on the Olympic stage. The 5,000m is less clear-cut, but when Yifter accelerates at 200m, no one can catch him. No wonder they call him 'Yifter the Shifter'.

Although the two greatest ever middle-distance runners were both British, the whole world thrilled to their long-awaited clash in the 1980 Olympics. The last time Steve Ovett and Sebastian Coe had met, in the 1978 European 800m, they had been so busy watching each other that they allowed East German Olaf Beyer to steal the gold. But now they were in a class of their own, vying with each other over the previous year in the setting of world records, while mutually avoiding a direct confrontation. Moscow, then, was to be the scene of the 'shoot-out'.

Their first encounter was the 800m, in which Coe was the world-record holder. The taller, stronger Ovett was renowned as a supreme racer, a master of tactics with the ability to elbow and barge his way out of trouble if the going got rough. And he possessed a cobra-like finish. Coe had a more sustained finish, but he was less robust than his rival, and virtually untested in a rough-and-tumble race.

In the 800m final, Coe proceeded to run the worst tactical race of his life. So concerned, it seemed, to avoid bodily contact, he was at the back and running wide at the bell. Ovett himself was boxed in, and had Coe 'gone' then, he would surely have won. But Ovett managed to extricate himself, and smoothly accelerated past Nikolai Kirov for an easy victory. Coe woke up in time to catch the Russian, but could make little impression on the winner.

Before the 1,500m final, Ovett had compiled a three-year run of 45 straight victories over 1,500m and a mile. And although the two Britons share the world record, Ovett is a clear favourite to win his second gold medal. Coe, in effect, is virtually written off as a racer.

The East German Jurgen Straub takes the field through a slow first two laps, tracked closely by Coe. Suddenly Straub 'goes' — and a grateful Coe goes with him. He feels confident that he can beat anyone in a sustained two-lap burst. He 'takes' the East German as they hit the home straight, and makes for the line. Ovett realizes he cannot catch Coe, and he does not lift himself to beat Straub. As Coe crosses the line, the strain, not only of the race but of the last six days, shows on his face. But he has answered his critics. As well as a world-record breaker, he is also a winner.

111

The Race of His Life

Crippled horse and dying jockey come back to win Grand National

Bob Champion rides Aldaniti to glory in the 1981 Grand National.

The Grand National is perhaps the most famous horse race in the world, a gruelling 4½-mile (7.2km) steeplechase with 30 formidable fences and a long history rich in tales of triumph and tragedy. And in 1981, a horse and his jockey joined the long list of legends and heroes, when Bob Champion rode Aldaniti up the long finishing straight to a four-length victory.

There have been many more dramatic finishes to the National, and more sensational races. Starting at 10–1, Aldaniti and Champion were second favourites. But go back 18 months in time, and the odds against this partnership riding in a race of any kind again, let alone winning the National, would have been astronomical. It was in August 1979 that Champion, 31 and a leading National Hunt jockey for several years, was told he was dying of cancer. He had perhaps as little as eight months to live. But as a result of American research in the seventies, there was a possible cure for his condition, by means of chemotherapy. The process involved several cycles of treatment — intravenous injections of liquid platinum — that were not only an ordeal in themselves but produced side effects that played havoc with the body systems and functions. There were times when even this courageous, strong-willed Yorkshireman felt like capitulating. What kept him going was the thought of riding again, and most of all it was a driving ambition to ride Josh Gifford's big chestnut Aldaniti in the National.

Meanwhile Aldaniti himself had broken down — for the second time. Having previously lost a year of his jumping career with a chipped bone in a hind fetlock, he had suffered a crippling tendon injury and needed firing operations on both forelegs. Trainer Gifford feared he would never race again. While Aldaniti was recovering slowly and quietly in a Sussex field, Champion was in America building up his wasted muscles. His cure had left him as weak as a child, and it was a long uphill struggle to fitness.

Gifford did a marvellous job on Aldaniti, and Champion rode the 11-year-old to a brilliant victory at Ascot in February 1981. But this was his only race in 18 months. How would he fare at Aintree? Well, after an error at the first fence, he settled down and took the lead at the end of the first circuit. There was a moment in the finishing straight when the favourite Spartan Missile looked dangerous, but Champion and Aldaniti drew clear again for a fairytale victory.

Shergar's Derby

Before the first Derby was run, in 1780, there was a great horse called Eclipse. He was so superior to his contemporaries that the famous phrase was coined: 'Eclipse first — the rest nowhere'. And this came to mind at Epsom in 1981, when 19-year-old Walter Swinburn, riding in his first Derby, rode the Aga Khan's Shergar to a 10-length victory easing up. It was the greatest winning margin in the history of the race.

Villa's Winner

Cup final flop scores dramatic replay goals

Of the two Argentinian World Cup stars who joined Spurs in 1978, Osvaldo Ardiles made the greater impression. An all-action player, he settled down at the heart of the side and enjoyed immense popularity. The erratic Ricardo Villa, on the other hand, an exciting midfield marauder, did not appear to number consistency among his virtues.

A bearded six-footer with a fine body swerve and a powerful shot, he scored some thrilling goals — but not often enough, and he lost his place more than once. Injury forced him out of the early rounds of the Cup in 1981, but as Spurs drove towards the final he won his place back, and scored a cracker in the semi-final replay against Wolves.

In the final, however, his form appeared to have deserted him once again, and he was pulled off after 68 minutes, with Spurs a goal down to Manchester City. He trudged off to the dressing-room in tears. His season, apparently, was over.

But Spurs equalized and forced a replay. Even so, it showed a great deal of courage on the part of their manager Keith Burkinshaw to keep faith with Villa and include him in the team again. And the big Argentinian repaid him

promptly, with a goal in seven minutes, sweeping the ball confidently into the net as it rebounded from a City defender. Forgotten was the lack-lustre performance on that same Wembley pitch five days earlier. This night, he was a new man.

It was not all Spurs, however, and City equalized and then surprisingly took the lead with a penalty in the second half. Spurs continued to press, though, and Garth Crooks fired home a well-deserved equalizer after 70 minutes.

The stage was set for the climax. Tony Galvin made a fine run up the left, pulled the ball back and slipped it inside to Villa. Brim-full of confidence now, the Argentinian ran at the City defence. The hearts began to pound in the Tottenham enclosures, because the fans knew what he was like in this mood. City's central defender Tommy Caton knew the danger, too, and forced Villa outside. Villa eased the ball past Caton and another defender before swerving inside to cut it back past Caton again. He seemed to delay his shot agonizingly for a split second, before slamming the ball joyfully past the advancing Corrigan. It was a fitting goal to win a classic 100th Cup final.

Top to bottom: **Villa takes the ball past Ranson (2) and Caton before swerving back inside and shooting past the despairing tackle of Caton and the helpless keeper.**

Davis wins World Snooker title

The name of Davis is synonymous with snooker. For it was the great Joe Davis who turned it into a world game in the 1920s, won the first world championship in 1927, and proceeded to beat allcomers until he retired from championship play in 1946. His brother Fred, too, was a three-time world champion.

Now there is another Davis on the world championship trophy — Steve — no relation, but at 23 with the promise of just as illustrious a career as his

famous namesakes. He came to the 1981 world championships at Sheffield as favourite, after a fine run of success in major competitions. He beat three former champions — Alex Higgins, Terry Griffiths, and Cliff Thorburn — to reach the final, where he was far too good for Doug Mountjoy. Because of his concentration at the table, he earned a reputation as an ice-cold executioner, but the tears of joy in his moment of triumph refuted any such notions.

The Fall and Rise of Ian Botham

Botham pulls the Ashes out of the fire

Fallen hero Ian Botham was at his lowest ebb. England had gone 12 matches without a win since he took over the captaincy, and his own form had gone to pieces — with bat and ball and even in the field. Here was the great all-rounder who had reached 1,000 runs and 100 wickets in fewer Tests than any other man — and the critics were calling for his head. After an unhappy tour of the West Indies, he had retained the captaincy only on a one-match basis. The first Test against Australia was lost, and although the second was drawn, Botham's personal contribution to the England batting was a 'pair'. Forestalling the selectors, Botham resigned the captaincy. Mike Brearley was recalled to lead England, and it was hoped that he might once more be able to bring the best out of Botham. That was the scenario for the third Test, at Headingly, in July 1981.

Australia batted first, and Botham's once-reliable fielding had not improved — he dropped two catches. Nevertheless, he took 6 for 95 as Australia declared at 401 for 9, and then 'top-scored' with 50 in England's miserable reply of 174. The next time he came in to bat, England were struggling to avoid an innings defeat. Soon they were 135 for 7, still 92 runs behind. And that's when the remarkable story of Botham's series really begins.

He set about the bowling with controlled violence, mixing the thoroughbred with the unorthodox. Graham Dilley contributed a swashbuckling 56, his maiden Test 50, in a stand of 117, Chris Old 29 out of 67, and Willis, while scoring only 2, helped Botham put on a priceless 37 runs for the last wicket. Botham, majestic and dominating, was unbeaten on 149, his highest Test score. Whatever happened now, he had revived the series and was once again a national hero.

Still, Australia needed only 130 to win, and appeared to be cruising serenely to their target at 56 for 1. Then

Left: **Botham, powerful and majestic, during his heroic Headingly knock.**

'Bustling Bob' Willis has Dyson caught at the wicket, and Australia, at 68 for 6, are on the way to sensational defeat at Headingly.

another hero took the stage: Bob Willis. Rejuvenated by Botham's heroics, he pounded up to the crease with new-found passion. The wickets began to tumble. He plundered 3 for 0 in 11 balls before lunch. After the break, he continued in the same vein. Australia were all out for 111. And Willis, another English star who had been written off, had produced his best ever Test figures of 8 for 43.

It was only the second time in Test history that a side had won after following on, and the first time this century. England were level and the

series was alive again.

In the fourth Test, Botham then proceeded to take Australia's last 5 wickets for 1 run when they needed only 37 to win. And then at Old Trafford he scored a glorious 118 to put England on their way to another victory when they were struggling.

So England had retained the Ashes. The sixth Test was a high-scoring, irrelevant draw, and Botham, who took his 200th Test wicket, did not need his 10 for 253 to win the 'Man of the Series' award. And what a series! What a man!

Australian Heroes

Although Botham dominated the series, there were some notable Australian performances, too. Terry Alderman took 9 wickets on his test début, and his series haul of 42 was a record for Australia against England. Dennis Lillee took 39 wickets. Allan Border hit a gallant 123 not out at Old Trafford with a broken finger. And Dirk Wellham made a début century at the Oval.

Botham bowls Alderman to wrap up the Edgbaston Test with a 5 for 1 spell.

Other great moments and exploits of the eighties

Jon Erikson, 26-year-old American, became the first person to swim the English Channel 3 times non-stop, in August 1981. Holder of the 2-way record (first set by his father, Ted), he first swam the Channel at 14, then a record.

Teofilio Stevenson, Cuban heavyweight, won his 3rd consecutive Olympic title in 1980.

Tom Watson won his 2nd US Masters in 1981, his 5th 'big four' title since 1975.

David Graham became, in 1981, the first Australian to win the US Open Golf Championship.

Hanni Wenzel won Liechtenstein's first Olympic gold medals when she took the two slaloms at Lake Placid. She also won a silver in the downhill, and her brother Andreas a silver in the men's downhill.

John McEnroe, 'superbrat' of tennis, finally ended Bjorn Borg's Wimbledon reign, beating him in 4 sets in the 1981 final — after more disgraceful displays of tantrums in earlier rounds.

Geoff Hunt of Australia, four times world squash champion, won the British Open Championship for a record eighth time in 1981.

Irena Rodnina of Russia won her 3rd successive pairs skating Olympic title in 1980.

Bruce Penhall won the 1981 World Speedway Championship, the first American since 1937.

Nelson Piquet of Brazil drove to 5th place in the US Grand Prix in great pain, to earn the vital 2 points that gave him the 1981 World Drivers Championship by a point.

Alberto Salazar, 23-year-old Cuban-born American, led a field of 16,000 to win the 1981 New York Marathon, in a world best time of 2hr 8min 13sec.

Index